The Alternate Reality News Service's Guide To Love, Sex and Robots

Ira Nayman

CONTENTS

ACKNOWLEDGMENTS

I would like to dedicate this book to all of the men, women and greebleflorps who dare to dream of happy ice cream when the twin moons are full and the tides sing to us of our better selves. And, of course, the political infrastructure that makes this all possible.

Oh, and terrific illustrator S. M. Carriere; Dispatcher, Zaphrod and kaedance, real people who asked fake questions; my supportive parents and family; and, as always, Web Goddess Gisela McKay.

Thanks everybody!

1. INTRODUCTION

Love, Sex and Robots:
An Alternate Reality News Service Forum

The Alternate Reality News Service asked three of its senior advice columnists to meet to discuss their role in times of social and technological brouhaha. Amritsar Al-Falloudjianapour writes about love and romance and technology. The Tech Answer Guy writes about technology and everything except love and romance. The Language Corrector Dude, well, it should be pretty obvious what he writes about.

The Language Corrector Dude: Actually, you would have been more correct in your usage of English if you had written: what he writes about should be pretty obvious.

You see? The forum was moderated by Alternate Reality News Service Editrix-in-Chief Brenda Brundtland-Govanni.

1.

Brenda Brundtland-Govanni: Let's get this over with as quickly as possible – I have a public editing at four. Now that we've plunged headfirst into the empty pool of the 21st century, what value, if any, do you think people find in advice columns?

Amritsar Al-Falloudjianapour: Oh, advice columns are stunningly important. In the 12th century, all people had to worry about was who their parents wanted them to marry and how to avoid the plague – sometimes both at once. As society has grown more complex, and we've developed a lot of more exotic illnesses, it has become harder and harder for the average person to find a path to a happy and fulfilling life. And, that doesn't even take into account cat to human translators! As the human race strolls blindly, if somewhat astringently, into an increasingly technology-dominated world, advice givers are more important than ever!

The Tech Answer Guy: I just try to keep dumb people from making dumb mistakes.

The Language Corrector Dude: I, uhh, I don't understand what I'm doing here. I mean, that wasn't a language question.

Brundtland-Govanni: We needed a fourth to make the panel more impressive. Also, we may play bridge if we have a spare few minutes after we're done. Just answer the question as best you can.

The Language Corrector Dude: Uhh, okay, well...new technologies – like Twitter, right? People experiment with language, and…and they need somebody to slap them down when they get too…creative. Somebody to remind them how to, you know, write proper.

The Tech Answer Guy: You? Hunh. Nice bowtie!

The Language Corrector Dude: Have respect for the Monarch!

The Tech Answer Guy: I have lots of respect for the Monarch! I ooze respect for the ferking Monarch out of every orifice of my body! Only, I never imagined the Queen being orange!

Amritsar Al-Falloudjianapour: Oh, aren't you just the pinnacle of sartorial splendour!

The Tech Answer Guy: Oh, yeah? Well I – you – what?

The Language Corrector Dude: Sartorial. Of or relating to a tailor, tailoring or tailored clothing. Splendour. Magnificent appearance or display. I think she was making fun of your jeans and – what do you call it?

Al-Falloudjianapour: On most men, it would be called a muscle shirt. On him, let's be generous and call it a lack of muscle shirt.

The Language Corrector Dude: And your lack of muscle -

The Tech Answer Guy: Okay. Yeah. I get it. I keep meaning to go to the gym, but there's always a Tim Hortons just before I get there. No matter what route I take, there's always a Tim Hortons. What can I say? All roads lead to –

Brundtland-Govanni: CAN WE GET BACK TO THE POINT HERE, PLEASE?

Al-Falloudjianapour: Which was…?

Brundtland-Govanni: Erm…the Internet is full of people who offer advice to others. What qualifies you to give advice more than them?

Al-Falloudjianapour: Anybody can give advice to anybody else. The question is, do you trust them to give you good advice? Trust is built on positive experience. So, you have to look at the experience of the person giving the advice. I am happy to say that, in over seventeen years of giving advice to Alternate Reality News Service readers, I have had only six of the people I advised commit suicide. Only six! That's a better suicide to years of service ratio than Dear Abby. Really! Look it up if you don't believe me!

The Tech Answer Guy: I have a miter saw.

Brundtland-Govanni: A miter saw?

The Tech Answer Guy: Absolutely. My mighty miter helps me cut through people's bullshit.

Brundtland-Govanni: I see. And, uhh, Language Corrector Dude?

The Language Corrector Dude: Oh. Uhh. I never thought about it, really. I guess…umm…I suppose it could be –

Al-Falloudjianapour: That you know things?

The Language Corrector Dude: Sure. I know things.

Al-Falloudjianapour: Things…other people don't know.

The Language Corrector Dude: Right. Right. I know things that other people don't know.

Al-Falloudjianapour: Aaaaboooouuuut…

The Language Corrector Dude: Oh! Of course. Language usage. I know things that other people don't know about language usage! You know – words and stuff.

2.

Brundtland-Govanni: What do you think is the major obstacle to people's happiness in our high tech world?

Al-Falloudjianapour: I think –

The Language Corrector Dude: What do you mean by "happiness?"

Brundtland-Govanni: What?

The Language Corrector Dude: Well, when you ask us about happiness, are you asking about the emotions experienced when in a state of well being? Or, are you asking about a state of well-being characterized by emotions ranging from contentment to intense joy?

Brundtland-Govanni: Umm…either one.

Al-Falloudjianapour: In that case —

The Language Corrector Dude: It's not that simple. Happiness is used in a variety of ways in a variety of contexts. Some people think that happiness is a warm puppy. Others thing that happiness is a warm gun. Still others think that happiness is a warm blartvogle.

Brundtland-Govanni: You wanna know how I would define happiness at this very moment?

The Language Corrector Dude: Yes.

Brundtland-Govanni: YOU SHUTTING THE FERK UP AND ALLOWING SOMEBODY ELSE TO ANSWER THE QUESTION!

The Tech Answer Guy smirks.

The Tech Answer Guy: Saw that one coming…

Brundtland-Govanni: Amritsar, you were about to say…?

Al-Falloudjianapour: I think that people make the mistake of thinking that technology will solve their emotional or relationship problems, and it simply doesn't work that way.

The Tech Answer Guy: Except for *Angry Firkins*.

Al-Falloudjianapour: I'm sorry?

The Tech Answer Guy: *Angry Firkins. Aaaaaaaaangry Fiiiiiirkiiiins*. Computer game. Highly addictive. Surely, you have heard of it.

Al-Falloudjianapour: Yes, I know what *Angry Firkins* is. What does it have to do with what I was saying?

The Tech Answer Guy: Tossing firkins at complex but highly unstable wooden structures allows players to release pent up aggression. That makes it much easier for them to deal with emotional or relationship problems. So, *Angry Firkins* is one technology that actually *does* help solve people's problems.

Al-Falloudjianapour: I hardly think that –

The Tech Answer Guy: Uh ah ah. According to "What the Ferk is a Firkin? Are Games Better Than Prozac, Or Should Researchers Take a Pill?" a peer reviewed article that was published in *FHM*, people who played the game were 97 per cent less likely to become depressed, alcoholics or Shriners.

Al-Falloudjianapour: Oh, really? What about...what about if nanobots in your toothpaste that are supposed to get rid of plaque actually turn your girlfriend into a rabid Three Stooges fan?

The Tech Answer Guy: Awkward. But, not insurmountable. Play an hour of *Angry Firkins*, and you'll start to see the artistry in the Three Stooges yourself.

Al-Falloudjianapour: What if you're the captain of a starship that comes across a planet with a new, peaceful form of intelligent life? All of your crew are very excited, of course, but within days of making first contact every member of the alien race is dead, and you don't know who to apologize to for bringing the microbes that killed them to the planet. What about that?

The Tech Answer Guy: Piece a cake. After a couple of hours playing *Angry Firkins*, you decide to plant evidence in their computer systems that the aliens were planning on attacking Earth. So, when you get home, instead of facing charges of genocide, you're actually a hero for killing them all.

Al-Falloudjianapour: Okay.

The Tech Answer Guy: That the best you got?

Al-Falloudjianapour: Oh, I'm just getting started. What if somebody developed a computer programme that allowed him – it's always a him who comes up with these ideas – to see light bulbs going off above people's heads in a display in his smart glasses. Not only does it do that, but it actually sends Alfred waves to the person he's looking at, which causes the person to come up with the design for a keyboard that would allow even an autistic chimpanzee to type 500 words a minute.

So, you're just walking along, minding your own business, wondering how long you will be able to keep your spouse in the dark about your *Jersey Shore* obsession, when – POW! OUT OF THE BLUE you come up with this new keyboard design. And, you have no idea what to do with it. After all, you're not an inventor. Or a zookeeper. This just makes you angry and confused. Will playing *Angry Firkins* help you out?

The Tech Answer Guy: Hmm. I have to think about that one. Oh, no, I don't. The answer is yes. After three hours of playing the game, you'll get in touch with a patent attorney who will advise you on how much money you can make off your invention. Oh, and I think you got the name of the brainwaves that cause you to be calm and creative wrong. They're Alfredo waves.

The Language Corrector Dude: Actually –

Al-Falloudjianapour: Well, uhh, alright, then. I guess *Angry Firkins* is a technology that does actually help people solve their problems. Still, most technologies do not.

The Tech Answer Guy: Actually –

Al-Falloudjianapour: Most. Technologies. Do. Not.

The Tech Answer Guy: Agreed.

3.

Brundtland-Govanni: One subject that hasn't come up yet is sex. Now –

The Language Corrector Dude: Oh, no. No, no, no, no, no. I don't – just no.

Al-Falloudjianapour: Sex is an important part of any healthy romantic relationship, Dude.

The Language Corrector Dude: Oh, god! Oh, god! Oh, god! Oh, god!

The Tech Answer Guy: Dude! Uncool!

The Language Corrector Dude: No words can convey – oh, god! Oh, god! Oh –

Brenda Brundtland-Govanni slaps The Language Corrector Dude. Long, stunned pause.

Brundtland-Govanni: This is the part where you're supposed to say, "Thanks. I needed that."

The Language Corrector Dude: Oh, god! Oh, god! Oh, god!

Brundtland-Govanni: (over him) Yet another example of movies lying to us! If I didn't enjoying slapping people for the feeling of flesh on flesh...!

The Language Corrector Dude: (moans) Oh, god! Oh, god! Oh, god!

Al-Falloudjianapour: Dude! Do you have a happy place?

The Language Corrector Dude: Oh, god! Oh, god! Oh, god!

Al-Falloudjianapour: (louder) Dude! DO YOU HAVE A HAPPY PLACE?

The Language Corrector Dude: A happy...place?

Al-Falloudjianapour: Do you have one?

The Language Corrector Dude: Sure. The, uhh, the Library of Congress.

The Tech Answer Guy: Figures.

Brundtland-Govanni: Watch it! The slapping glove does not discriminate!

The Tech Answer Guy: Sorry.

Al-Falloudjianapour: I want you to go there now while we talk about…what you don't want to talk about. Can you do that for me?

The Language Corrector Dude: O…okay.

Brundtland-Govanni: Okay. I'm wondering what role new technologies play in se – I mean, human se – uhh…human doing it.

Al-Falloudjianapour: Well! Human…you know is a very fraught subject. It –

The Tech Answer Guy: Hee hee. You said frott.

Al-Falloudjianapour: There's nothing dirty about the word fraught!

The Tech Answer Guy: There is when it's the start of frottage.

Al-Falloudjianapour: If I had intended to say that human sexuality is –

The Language Corrector Dude: (moaning) Oh, eighteenth century first edition of Lawrence Sterne's *Shirley, A Milke Maide's Taile*, is there nothing you can't teach us about the perfect form of the novel?

Al-Falloudjianapour: If I had meant to say…it was a frottage subject, I would have said it was a frottage subject! But, I didn't, did I?

Brundtland-Govanni: And, the point you were trying to make was…?

Al-Falloudjianapour: I think that there are a lot of factors in why people do or do not get se – physi – umm, why they don't enjoy doing it as much as they could. Pressure to perform, obviously. A lack of basic understanding of how to please a partner. Other –

The Tech Answer Guy: Hey! I've never had any complaints!

Al-Falloudjianapour: Was I talking about you?

The Tech Answer Guy: You were – looking – eye contact – never mind.

Al-Falloudjianapour: Other psychological issues can get in the way of pleasure. There –

The Language Corrector Dude: (to himself) Twenty-seven copies of *Murder on the Orient Express*? That seems a tad excessive…

Al-Falloudjianapour: Gritting my teeth, I continue. There are so many factors that contribute to bad…getting it on. I would caution people against adding technology to the list.

The Tech Answer Guy: Balls!

Al-Falloudjianapour: Lovely.

Brundtland-Govanni: Tech Answer Guy?

The Tech Answer Guy: Anything that makes it easier for people to get jiggy with each other is fine by me!

4.

Brundtland-Govanni: Lately, I have noticed a lot of articles coming into the newsroom about people having relationships with robots. Is cyborg love the next step in human evolution, or a dead end for the species that alienates us from other human beings by encouraging seemingly deep but ultimately sterile relationships with objects that project the illusion of emotional depth without actually possessing it?

Al-Falloudjianapour: What a thoughtful and, if I may say so, insightful question! There are many –

The Tech Answer Guy: You wrote that question yourself, didn't you?

Al-Falloudjianapour: …ways of approaching – what? That's irrelevant.

The Tech Answer Guy: She wrote the question herself.

The Language Corrector Dude: It's obvious.

Al-Falloudjianapour: IT DOESN'T MATTER WHO WROTE THE BLOODY QUESTION!

The Tech Answer Guy: Definitely her.

The Language Corrector Dude: Absolutely.

Brundtland-Govanni: Okay, enough of that. Let Amritsar answer her question.

The Tech Answer Guy: (under his breath) Told you.

Al-Falloudjianapour: Ahem… Some people are too shy, too socially awkward to develop romantic relationships with other people. Psychiatrists have a term for this: Too Shy and Socially Awkward to Develop Romantic Relationships Syndrome. Seriously. It's in the *DSM VI, Director's Cut*. Relating to machines arguably gives them a measure of emotional comfort and connectedness that they wouldn't otherwise be able to achieve. To this extent, it's a good thing.

The problem, though, is that people without Too Shy and Socially Awkward to Develop Romantic Relationships Syndrome could use machines in ways that retard – and, I use the word in its clinical sense, so, please, no letters – their relationships with other people. A man who is always fighting with his wife about which denture adhesive she uses could withdraw from their relationship into the arms of their AI-enhanced washing machine. This would –

The Language Corrector Dude: There's nothing wrong with talking to your AI-enhanced washing machine.

Al-Falloudjianapour: I…I beg your pardon?

The Language Corrector Dude: Sometimes, a washing machine can understand your problems better than a human partner can. Washing machines have a simple wisdom that cuts through the nonsense of everyday life and quickly gets to something profound. I mean, all life is ultimately just a cycle of wash-rinse-wash-dry repeat, isn't it? Besides, washing machines are terrific listeners.

Long pause.

Al-Falloudjianapour: Okay. Umm…okay. Thanks for that. You know, Dude, maybe you and I should have a long talk when this forum is finished…

Brundtland-Govanni: Tech Answer Guy – your thoughts on…umm…whatever we were supposed to be talking about?

The Tech Answer Guy: Yeah, well, first off, let me just say that what a man does with a washing machine in the privacy of his own home is nobody else's business.

The Language Corrector Dude: Or a laundromat.

The Tech Answer Guy: A what?

The Language Corrector Dude: What a man does with a washing machine in the privacy of his own laundromat is nobody else's business.

The Tech Answer Guy: Do you own the laundromat?

The Language Corrector Dude: No. Is that important?

Pause.

The Tech Answer Guy: Secondly, as more and more of us get prosthetic enhancements, the line between human being and machine blurs. Now, I ain't saying it's gonna be erased completely or nothing. I'm just saying.

Brundtland-Govanni: Still, Tech Answer Guy…robots?

The Tech Answer Guy: Aww, people get emotionally attached to all sorts of shit. Pets. Money. Andy Warhol lithographs. At least artificial intelligence enhanced robots can give something back to them. Or, if that don't float yer boat, look at it this way: a robot ain't nothin' but a vibrator with legs.

The Language Corrector Dude: Aah ah! Codex! Dewey decimal system! CARDBOARD COVEEEEEERRRRRRRS!

5.

Al-Falloudjianapour: (quietly) Remember: deep breaths. In and out. In and out…

Brundtland-Govanni: So, panelists: final words?

The Language Corrector Dude: Obsolescence. Defenestration. Pudding. Post-recreational stress disorder. Oh, and…and…it's on the tip of my – TONGUE!

Al-Falloudjianapour: That's it?

The Language Corrector Dude: She asked me for last words.

Al-Falloudjianapour: Are you always so literal?

The Language Corrector Dude: It's what I do.

Brundtland-Govanni: Amritsar – last words?

Al-Falloudjianapour: L'enfer, c'est les autre ecrivains!

The Language Corrector Dude: Can you repeat that in English?

Al-Falloudjianapour: Oh, you'd like that, wouldn't you?

The Language Corrector Dude: As a matter of fact –

Brundtland-Govanni: Tech Answer Guy?

The Tech Answer Guy: Shouldn't we let them finish?

Brundtland-Govanni: Any. Final. Words?

The Tech Answer Guy: Uhh. Yeah. Sure. Okay. Be good to each other and your garden tools. You may not always have each other, but you'll always have to kill weeds. Bastards.

Brundtland-Govanni: Great. Thanks, everybody.

Pause.

Brundtland-Govanni: Okay, Looks like I've got an hour to kill – wanna cut for partners?

2. GIRLS

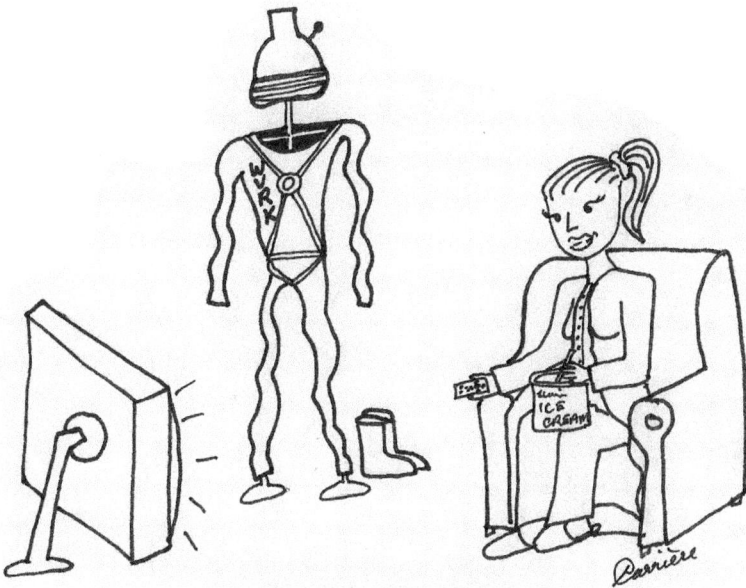

ROCHELLE DIDN'T REGRET GIVING UP THE VIRTUAL ORGY TO WATCH A `SEX AND THE CITY' MARATHON.

Ask Amritsar: Unanswerable Questions

Dear Amritsar,

Our baby daughter has my eyes and my husband Philbert's nose. She has uncle Guido's hair (he always had great hair, even when there wasn't very much of it left on his head) and auntie Modrolla's ears, nose and throat (she specialized). Our daughter has the cutest spleen thanks to grandpa Aguilar (he may have been a right bastard, but he had the most photogenic spleen you've ever seen) and, when she grows into them, will have aunt Zelda's breasts (I know, I know, Zelda had been excommunicated from the family because of the tortellini incident, but, really, that was over 40 years ago and, anyway, she fed nine children with those breasts and they still looked fabulous, so we knew our daughter just had to have them). We tried to give her my brother's elbows, but he doesn't believe in science – I know, right? In this day and age! But, he does live in a shack in the country without electricity or a Nintendo WII, so I guess at least he's not hypocritical about it – so we had to settle for my husband's cousin Elmorrie's less perfect but still pretty amazing elbows. Uncle Guido (again) gave our baby her big toes (you'd be surprised at how difficult it is to find really cute big toes!). From my cousin Penelopea, she got her aorta (Penelopea, may she rest in peace, lived to 102 despite smoking like a chimney – she had a set of lungs on her that could drop a rhino at 200 feet!) And, of course, she has Albert Einstein's IQ and Benny Hill's sense of humour.

What should we name her?

Jessica Philomena Eroica Janet Planet Majors Alison Catchall-Dumbrowski

Hey, Babe

Genetic engineering has really come a long way, hasn't it?

Shakespeare once said, "What's in a name?" It took over 300 years, but a *Fortune* survey of truly stinking rich people finally came up with an answer: three to five million dollars and a shot at the CEO's office. According to the magazine, names to embrace: Biff, Todd, Gil and James. Names to avoid: Slappy, Gomez, Dinette and Pol Pot.

Given this, I think you will agree that the name you give your child is very important. (Of course, according to most sources other than *Fortune*, a female child will only make 72 per cent of what a male child will make, but, if she has a really weird name, she'll make even less, so the general principle holds better than Krazy Glu.)

There are a number of approaches you could try to naming your daughter that recognize the various people who contributed their genetic material to her. For example, you could build a name out of the initials of all of them: J from your name, P from your husband's name, G from your uncle's name, and so on. If you do this, you get: Jpgmazepab. Hmm…it could be…Serbian.

Or, here's an idea: use an **anagram** of the initials of all of the people who donated their etc. This could give you the name…Bappazjegm! Or, perhaps, Zjappegamb. There: many people would consider that name Polish. In a dimly lit room… If they didn't look at it too closely…

Another possible way of finding a name for your child would be to combine objects that have special significance for each of the people who donated their you know the drill. You, for instance, might really like roses. Your husband might collect pipe cleaners. For uncle Guido, it could be an old teddy bear. And, so on. This would yield a name like: Rose Pipe Cleaner Teddy Machette iPod Iris Grenade Lioness

Dreamcatcher Lily. Of course, you may want to choose your objects more carefully; according to *Fortune*, the name Lily is a real career killer.

Worthy approaches all. For myself, I would name your daughter Jane.

Dear Amritsar,

Why Jane?

Jessica Philomena Eroica Janet Planet Majors Alison Catchall Dumbrowski

Hey, Babe,

Why not Jane?

Dear Amritsar,

Where is the life we have lost in the living?

Tom Eliot

Hey, Babe,

It's dropped behind the couch in the den. Really, Tom, if you would just take better care of the life we have lost in the living, you wouldn't lose track of it so easily!

Send your relationship problems to the Alternate Reality News Service's *sex, love and technology columnist at questions@lespagesauxfolles.ca. Amritsar Al-*

Falloudjianapour is not a trained therapist, but she does know a lot of stuff. AMRITSAR SAYS: I don't want to tell you how to run your life, but, you know, maybe I do, just a little.

Ask Amritsar: No Such Thing as an Original Sin

Dear Amritsar,

When my parents tell me to programme the housekeeperbot to take out the trash, I do it without question. I always finish my homework before I post anonymous comments to *Gillligan's Island* Farcebook fan pages. I always eat my vegetables, even when they are unidentifiable green lumps that were grown on the moons of Jupiter. In short, I like to think of myself as a "good girl."

At least, that was before my family got a Home Universe Generator™.

As a reward for my good behaviour, my parents allowed me to watch the Home Universe Generator™ for an hour every evening (and, because I am who I am, I never begged them for more time). I thought I would look in on my life in other dimensions, you know, to pick up tips on how to be a better daughter, friend and citizen.

Well! In the first universe I looked at, I was making out with Rance Delectus! I mean, his hands were all over me – it was like he was waxing a car or something! Don't get me wrong – Rance is the quarterback of the football team at More Science High School and Research Lab – he would be quite the catch! But, of course, I mean in a state sanctioned civil arrangement, and I did not see rings on either of our fingers. When I groped his groin, I had to turn off the Home Universe Generator™ and catch my breath – hard to imagine how *that* was going to make me a better citizen!

After a couple of minutes, I tried another dimension. Well, well! In that one, I was making out with Jeremiah Jedediah! He moved his hands around my body with considered, measured strokes, like he was planning out moves in a chess match, which makes sense considering he was the Chess Club Czar. Gross! I would rather lock lips with a vacubot exhaust than kiss him in my universe – I guess the other me had lower standards! When I groped *his* groin, I had to turn off the Home Universe Generator™ in disgust – I can't believe I thought that that was a winning move!

I decided to try one more dimension. Well, well, well! There I was, making out with Vida Lou Buttram. I know, right? Only the head of the cheerleading squad for the More Science High Flying Lab Rats football team (they were named after an experiment in jet propulsion went horribly wrong – still, science's loss was our football team's gain!)! Only the most desired woman in the entire school! Now, I've never been attracted to other girls, so when I groped **her** groin...I had to watch for another few minutes just to be sure I fully understood what I was seeing.

Oh, Amritsar, I'm a slut and I didn't even know it! How is such a thing possible?

Terpsichore Condiment

Hey, Babe,

Okay, take a deep breath. You don't want to hyperventilate and pass out before I've had the opportunity to share my hard-won wisdom with you. Are you sitting comfortably? Good.

To begin, let me just say that Amritsar is not keen on the term "slut." As you know, it started as a Scandinavian word, "sluttavoisk," meaning, "cheese woman." In Victorian England, this became shortened to mean, "potential victim of

Jack the Ripper." Since Victorians found it hard to pronounce "avoisk," the word was relengthened and reshortened to "slutt." Of course, it became the word we know today when it lost its terminal "t" during the Second World War due to letter rationing.

As for your little problem, well (sorry, but, unlike you, I don't feel the need to go to the well more than once), I believe you are making too much of what you have seen. The Terpsichores you watched clearly made different choices in their lives in their realities than you have in yours.

That doesn't mean that, in this universe, you are a Scandinavian cheese woman. Some women have allergies to dairy products. Some women had bad experiences with emmental and have sworn off all cheeses as a result. Some women just don't like the concept of milk products combined with mold. The important thing is that, no matter what other versions of you in other universes may do, you don't have to partake of the cheeseboard of life until you are ready.

Send your relationship problems to the Alternate Reality News Service's *sex, love and technology columnist at questions@lespagesauxfolles.ca. Amritsar Al-Falloudjianapour is not a trained therapist, but she does know a lot of stuff. AMRITSAR SAYS: don't challenge me on English etymology. I sleep with a dictionary under my pillow, and, when I wake up with a headache, I spend hours studying the words that have caused me such grief!*

Ask Amritsar About the Irresistible Impulse

Dear Amritsar,

The other night I had a date with a smoking hot woman, Beverly Bitmap. I am not exaggerating, either: the fire department checked in with her every hour just to be sure she hadn't set any buildings on fire. Trying to impress her, I took Bev (she asked me call her that…well, that was the compromise we came up with, anyway) to Stubby's Stabby Steakery, a British/Somali fusion restaurant.

We ordered drinks and Bev excused herself and went to the bathroom. Then, we ordered dinner and Bev went to the bathroom again. After the drinks arrived, she went to the bathroom once more. Then, again, after her first bite of soup. Bev went to the bathroom four times during the actual meal (salad, steak, steak after it was sent back to be cooked a little more, steak after it had returned from being cooked a little more), then, again, after ordering dessert, then twice more while we were having dessert (once after she sent the chocolate mousse back to be cooked a little more and once after the chocolate mousse had returned from being cooked a little more). She is currently in the bathroom as I write this while waiting for the bill.

I may not know a lot about women, but even I can see a pattern emerging.

Should I assume that Bev has been going to the bathroom so often because she is checking her email, or should I just accept that she has an exceptionally weak bladder?

Baruch Boitano
from his blueberry

Hey, Babe,

Women go to the bathroom for a variety of reasons. Sure, sometimes they check their email. Others times, they play a couple levels of *Bejeweled*. Other other times, they update their Farcebook pages. Sometimes they tweet about the terrible conversation you are making (HINT: talking about the infighting among the members of your pet rock collection isn't going to stoke anybody's ardour flames). Once in a while, they listen to the latest Autotunes song on YahooTube. Once in an even longer while, they check their calendar to see if they haven't mistaken the date with you for an appointment with their dentist.

Sometimes, and I know this may be hard to believe but you're just going to have to trust me on this one, women go to the bathroom because they have to pee.

Given all of these possibilities, I can understand why you might have difficulty knowing what your date is up to. I would suggest that you honestly assess whether your dinner conversation is so dull it would freeze Husain Bolt in mid-sprint. Unfortunately, most of us are not very good at assessing the quality of our dinner conversation; fortunately, there's an app for that.

Date Deathwatch ($3.97 from The Apple Schnorrer) is simple: enter the age of your date, the place where you expect to have the conversation and the topic you would like to discuss. DD compares these inputs to its database and returns an assessment of your choice of conversation on a scale of one ("Spring for some champagne, Casanova!") to 17 ("Is your insurance paid up? Because you'll be lucky if your date doesn't try to strangle you with your own tie before the night is over!")

Date Deathwatch can give you a big clue to what your date is doing in the bathroom, but it can't tell you for certain.

For that, you would need the Toilet Treachery Tracker app ($3,970,003.97 from the Department of Defence Store). Simply enter the name of the establishment in which you are dining: T^3 uses the latest thermal imaging technologies to determine how many women are in the bathroom, then employs the latest signal capture and filtering algorithms to determine what, if any, electronic communications your date is engaging in. Owing to outdated concepts of privacy (and the laws that enable them), the T^3 app will only give you the name of the programme the woman is using, not the actual content; but there are third party add-ons (ie: Date Spy, Date Stalker and Ultimate Date Creepiness) that can fill in this gap.

But, honestly, if your date wants to get away from you so badly that she spends more time in the bathroom than at the table, what else do you really need to know?

Send your relationship problems to the Alternate Reality News Service's *sex, love and technology columnist at questions@lespagesauxfolles.ca. Amritsar Al-Falloudjianapour is not a trained therapist, but she does know a lot of stuff. AMRITSAR SAYS: love hurts. To be on the safe side, get robopocalypse insurance.*

Ask Amritsar: When the Seltzerpuss Turns...

Dear Amritsar,

I work in the Poughkeepsie, Alberta offices of Transgalactic Puffballs Inc, an import/export company that deals mostly in artifacts from Tau Ceti. You know: self-basting Farrumph roast holders, hovering carpets ("For people who are scared of heights!"), Death Masks of Ramen the Inedible, that sort of thing. I've worked in the Fulfillment Department (a misnomer if I ever used one on letterhead!) for 12 years; I thought I would be stuck there until I clawed my eyes out with a stuffed eagle I keep on my desk or retired, whichever came last.

Then, Catherine Hakim made it okay for women to use their sexuality to get ahead in the workplace. Yay! Oh, I may have had to strangle my inner Gloria Steinem in order to follow Hakim's advice, but, honestly, she left cigarette butts all over my spleen, and I could swear that was a liquor stain on my lower intestine, so it was about time for her to go! Sure, I would be setting the cause of women back 60 years, but I could live with that – 50s fashions are so flattering to a woman's figure!

Look at it this way: if a man can dress to please his boss, if he always has a smile for his boss and he flirts shamelessly with his boss…well, he would have to be gay because there are still few women in positions of authority. Not that there's anything wrong with that. In any case, that relatively rare scenario is a good enough example for me to pattern my behaviour after!

So, I started wearing my most sensual clothes (you know – the ones I paid the most for even though they contain the least amount of fabric) and saving up money for the day when I could get my teeth whitened so I could smile more without being self-conscious about tooth rot™. There was only one problem.

My boss is a Seltzerpuss.

For those not familiar with Tau Cetians (Tau Cetaceans?) – and, since they like to keep a low profile (and, after the incident with the Armenian Ambassador and the Lobster Thermidor, who can blame them?), that's probably most of your readers – they are essentially six foot tall worms. With limbs. And, something approaching a face. Their faces are made up of two slits at a 90 degree angle above which sit two round holes – Scott McCloud would recognize them as faces, if nobody else.

My feminine wiles were completely wasted on Krrang-Facken, my boss. When I tried winking at him, for instance, he asked me, "Is your optical input device malfunctioning?" When I started coming to work in low cut blouses, he suggested I "cover up before you get a chest cold." One day, I patted an area opposite Krrang-Facken's face, about halfway down that, on a human body, would have been a butt; he avoided me in the office for the next three weeks.

Realizing that this approach wasn't working, I decided to meet Krrang-Facken on his own turf. I started wearing *Dior's Oligochaeta*, a perfume that smells like moist soil with just a hint of feces. No reaction. I started wearing makeup that made my skin look a shade of pale pink that came close to that of a Seltzerpuss. Nothing. I may as well have stuck a pair of firecrackers up my nose and sung *The Wizard of Oz Dark Side of the Moon* for all the good my efforts did me!

Do you have any idea about what I should try next? Because, frankly, I'm thinking of giving up the import-export business and becoming a gunman's moll!

Name Withheld By Request Because Mary Traverse Didn't Want To Be Held Up To Ridicule

Hey, Babe,

Funny thing about the Seltzerpuss: they reproduce asexually. When one is ready to have children, it is cut in half, and both halves grow to become fully formed adults. So, not only have you sold out your sisters, who will have to work five times as hard to work twice as hard to get half the recognition of a man, but you did so in a way that will get you absolutely nowhere.

It's women like you that make me embarrassed for my gender.

Send your relationship problems to the Alternate Reality News Service's *sex, love and technology columnist at questions@lespagesauxfolles.ca.* Amritsar Al-Falloudjianapour *is not a trained therapist, but she does know a lot of stuff. AMRITSAR SAYS: fad diets come and go, but Type 2 Diabetes is forever.*

Ask Amritsar About Obsolete Joys

Dear Amritsar,

I am happily married with three children, a pet cow named Oscar Meyer (our youngest, Willem, was a little unclear on where we get our meat from when he named her) and a mortgage that would make your ears bleed. Despite all the good things that I have managed to claw out of existence in this indifferent and unforgiving universe, I find myself fondly fantasizing about my college days.

In particular, I have become a little obsessed with a flash mob I was part of in my second year at Harrods Secret Shopper Academy. It's not that I think about it all of the time – I thought about wiener dogs a couple of days ago, for instance, and last week I spent almost a minute thinking about how different the world would have been if Harry Houdini had been a concert pianist.

The group met in the quad (just behind the student centre and below the belt – you know how young people are!). There were over 50 of us (that was the mob part). At the same moment, we stripped completely naked (that was the flash part) and lurched side to side like autistic robots faced with a paradox for 27.8 seconds (I found counting off the eighth of a second to be the hardest part). Then, humming "My Cherie Amour," we grabbed the clothes of the person to our right and ran off in all directions. I spent the rest of the day dressed like a garden gnome (I really should have found somebody taller to stand next to, but strange things happen to everybody's clothes their first time).

I have never felt so alive. Well, not without the risk of STDs and pregnancy, in any case.

The problem with flash mobs – other than goose bumps – maybe January wasn't the best time for it – is that you don't know anybody involved with them. Is there any way I can find out? I'd like to invite them out for coffee, or maybe a night of Stevie Wonder karaoke.

Jenny from the Hood Ornament

Hey, Babe,

Flash mobs – that was over a decade ago, right? I thought that they had something to do with a DC Comics hero, but obviously, I was mistaken.

Okay, give me a second…F-L-A-S-H M-O-B – no strange accents or silent letters? Good…okay, right – weird social phenomenon featuring strange public behaviour…un hunh…early manifestation of what was possible with new computer-aided communications technologies…right…I see…ended when all of the people who couldn't be embarrassed had already been part of one…right, right right – WITH A MELON?

Ahem. Okay. I have consulted experts on…this sort of thing, and they tell me that you are looking for a flash mob reunion. The experts – who would rather not be named because nobody gives tenure to anybody who studies obsolete technologies – except, of course, for English professors – claim that this desire is not uncommon.

In fact, according to one of my experts – no, seriously, you wouldn't even recognize his name if I – you're willing to take that chance? But…okay. Okay. My expert is…Ai Weiweipedia. He's…Chinese. Okay? Happy now? In fact, according to – you know what? This paragraph has been ruined for me. Let's start afresh in the next paragraph.

According, in fact, to one of my experts, there is a Flash Mob Clearing House Web page (http://www.fmch.urg/index.shhtml), where people who were once part of one can try to connect to other people who – no, wait, it just shut down because of a malware attack. But, the Flash Mob Clearing House's Farcebook fan page is still – no, hold on, the page has been reinstated, but now you have to sign in and verify your identity. Okay, so, if you want to find – oh, now a splinter group that doesn't like the new policy has started its own Web page – The Clearing House for Flash Mob Info page – that will remain open to anonymous posts.

Things really move fast on the Internet.

Okay, so, the point is that there are ways for you to connect with other people who may have been involved with your flash mob. But, do you rally want to relive your peak experience?

When I was…even younger than the young age I am now, I took a balloon tour of Europe. Ah, the misty spray on my face, the gentle swaying of the gondola, the bucolic landscapes below! This was a peak experience that I cherished for years.

Then, last year, I had the bright idea of reliving the experience. That misty spray? It was acid rain that left my skin blotchy and discoloured. The gentle swaying of the gondola? There isn't enough Dramamine in the world to settle my stomach! And, the bucolic landscapes? Shuttered factories and abandoned company towns aren't as romantic as they sound, even when viewed from several thousand feet in the air.

Believe me – the only thing that can come from a second peek at peak experiences is disappointment!

Send your relationship problems to the Alternate Reality News Service's *sex, love and technology columnist at questions@lespagesauxfolles.ca.* Amritsar Al-Falloudjianapour *is not a trained therapist, but she does know a lot of stuff. AMRITSAR SAYS: I often relive pique experiences, but that's a completely different matter, one that I am not prepared to share with the likes of you!*

Ask The Tech Answer Guy: How Do They Do It?

Yo, Tech Answer Guy,

I work in the fulfillment department of National Squidjelim and Dreams, Inc. This year's ChristmaKwaanzUkah had a festive "Gender Reversal" theme, where everybody was supposed to dress up like a member of the opposite sex. The fact that the company has only three female employees, and one of them, Agnieszka Maderios, was in charge of choosing the theme, should have set off warning bells in somebody's head, but it was a bad year for Dream fulfillment, and I guess we were grasping for whatever small measure of joy we could get.

A lot of people wore floral print dresses and called it a party. However, when I got my MBA, I had a minor in amateur theatrics, so I was steeped in Method Partying. I decided that if I was going to play the part of a woman for ChristmaKwaanzUkah, I was going to do it right, I was going to go the full Hoover.

35

What was I thinking? Being a woman is brutal!

They smear greasy goop all over their lips. They wear panty hose, which itch worse than army ants crawling between your thighs. They walk in six inch heels – I felt like the 57th floor of an office tower in a windstorm the whole time! They carry around one pound melons on their chests and wear constricting harnesses for them – I stooped for days after my ordeal! Not only that, but the things they do to get rid of unwanted hair would make Caligula run for his mommy!

How do they do it? I mean, I wept for three days, and I was only a woman for four hours. Day in and day out, year after year, for decades! CAN ANYBODY PLEASE GOD TELL ME HOW THEY DO IT?

Sincerely,
Dorian from Grey County

Yo, Dory,

You know, if you wanted to find out what women go through, you could have saved yourself a lot of trouble if you had just watched *Tootsie*. Not that I've ever seen it. Or, for that matter, *What Women Want*. Not that I've ever even heard of it or knew it existed.

How do women do it? Painkillers and millions of years of evolution, I would suspect.

The Tech Answer Guy

Yo, Tech Answer Guy,

That was pretty glib, wasn't it?

Evolution isn't really an explanation for why women spend so much time and energy on their looks. Men of the remote Appalachoogie Tribe in the Allegheny River basin paint their faces with jam made from the red Floozleberry and walk around on six inch stilts; in fact, the size of men's stilts is often correlated, rightly or wrongly, with the size of their noses. Then, they post pictures of themselves on Farcebook to attract mates.

Nor is this the only example. The wild bankers of the Plains of the Wall Street have elaborate costuming rituals that signal their status in the community. A man's gotta do what a man's gotta do, and sometimes that's gaudify himself to attract women.

This is a reflection of the natural world, where the males of species as wide-ranging as peacocks, bonobo monkeys and Ford Impalas use colourful displays to attract females. The burden we place on women to look a certain way in order to attract potential male mates is, therefore, a social construct, not unlike stock markets, tenant associations and the infield fly rule. Especially the infield fly rule.

In fact, some argue that the amount of pain society demands women suffer in order to be "beautiful" is related to how insecure men in that society feel about themselves. (That would be members of the Some Institute for Sociological Panjandrummation.) Given current economic conditions, and their attendant social upheavals, it's a miracle that women aren't required to wear rouge on their cheeks that's a mile thick!

As for painkillers, I prefer a good belt of Scotch in the morning, even though it's hard to drink off of – I can't begin to tell you how often I have poked myself in the eye with the buckle! My point is that men have our own methods of escaping the pain of our existence.

Sincerely,
Marcus from Pedantic City

Yo, Marky,

Glib is the new black.

The Tech Answer Guy

*If you are a dude with a question about the latest technology, ask The Tech Answer Guy by sending it to questions@lespagesauxfolles.ca. Just remember: the future is now...but it's all going wrong. Bodies good for nothing, but it's to nothing they – sorry. I was channeling my inner The for a moment. Which The? THE The. * SIGH * The Tech Answer Guy longs for the days when bands had simple, easy to comprehend names. You know, like Tangerine Dream, Fairport Convention or The Nazz...*

Ask Amritsar To Weight

Dear Amritsar,

I'm huge. Humongous. Humongo. Humo. Hum. Really, really big. A blimp on legs. I'm five foot nine inches tall and weigh almost 98 pounds. I'm Gina Ginormous!

I've had my tummy tuckered and my lips stapled. I spent a month only eating foods beginning with the letter "x." I was hypnotized to see the face of Clara Peller whenever I looked at a cake or a pastry. Nothing seemed to work.

Is there a technology so new that it doesn't even have a commercial name yet that can help me with this problem?

Chubby Chelios

Hey, Babe,

There's always a technology so new that it doesn't even have a commercial name yet that can help you with your problems. This is known as the Rathskeller Surmise, after the scientist who first proposed it after a long and successful career playing Sherlock Holmes in the movies. Unfortunately, you won't be able to afford it. This is the Reality Principle, named after Irwin Reality, the producer of all of those 1970s disaster movies.

Still, since you asked, the technology is described in official Convex Tech Mex Spex corporate specs as ALo234PlopPlopDoozies V2.35.4.1 Fuschia. According to CTMS, it is a pair of glasses that has digital lenses programmed to make food look bigger than it actually is while not affecting how the wearer views anything else.

This is how it works: the glasses make French fries look like 100 year-old tree trunks and hamburgers look like semi-detached two-bedroom homes with neo-faux traditional kitchen, post-modernist bathroom fixtures, combination den/woodworking shop and three quarters of a parking space. People wearing the glasses tend not to eat the fries because they are afraid the spooky spuds will be cut down by lumberjacks who don't yell "Timber" and crush them; naturally, they want to save their families the embarrassment of having to explain that they were killed by a falling French fry. Eaters tend to stay away from the burgers for fear that they will be bankrupted by the mortgage.

The glasses are programmed not to do this to healthy foods. Seeing celery the size of cabers might give eaters looking to lose weight the misimpression that the stalks could only be eaten by brawny people of Scottish descent. Seeing wobbly pieces of tofu the size of Hummers might give some people flashbacks to the blancmange invasion of 1970, forcing them to put paper bags over their heads until the people around them stepped into steamer trunks and sang "Jerusalem" at the tops of their lungs.

Trying to lose weight is difficult enough without getting the whole community involved!

Dear Amritsar,

I'm five foot three and weigh 237 pounds. My friends at Communist Martyrs High School all weigh over 300 pounds. My BFFFN (Best Friend Forever For Now), Rosamunda McWockwalk, weighs 417 pounds in a skimpy bikini. Not that anybody wants to see her in one. Anyhoo, she says we can't be friends unless I gain at least 100 pounds. I…I can't lose Rosamunda. She's the captain of he cheerleading squad – I would be kicked off it and forced to wander aimlessly around campus until somebody from the chess club took pity on me and asked me if I wanted to learn a thousand and one uses for a rook. I would never be able to live that down!

Is there a technology so new that it doesn't even have a commercial name yet that can help me with this problem?

Skinny Minneapolis

Hey, Babe,

There's always a technology so new that it doesn't even have a commercial name yet that can – where have I heard this before? No matter. Good advice, unlike good skin, is truly timeless.

You could also benefit from Convex Tech Mex Spex' ALo234PlopPlopDoozies V2.35.4.1 Fuschia. Once you have a pair of the glasses that are currently unavailable to the public (I don't judge), find a patch on the Internet (not, to be clear, the kind you would find on the *Girls with Eyepatches* Web site) that will reverse the polarity on the glasses. This will make food appear smaller than it actually is (but, astute reader, you were way ahead of me on this one, weren't you?).

T-bone steaks the size of your fingernail! A small mountain of mashed potatoes in the shape of Devil's Tower that appear to be the size of a molehill! Asparagus spears the size of toothpicks!

Darnit, but all this helping people is making me hungry!

Send your relationship problems to the Alternate Reality News Service's *sex, love and technology columnist at questions@lespagesauxfolles.ca. Amritsar Al-Falloudjianapour is not a trained therapist, but she does know a lot of stuff. AMRITSAR SAYS: making up your mind is a lot messier than making up your bed. No wonder so many people go to great lengths to avoid it!*

Ask Amritsar: You Can Jaclyn, But you Can't Heidi

Dear Amritsar,

I'm an ankle, tibia and spleen specialist at Toronto Generalissimo Hospital. My husband, I. L. Fiornello, plays tackle for the Maple Leafs. My two sons, Garrett and Tarregg, are past the age of being clingy, but haven't reached the age of being bitchy.

I have the ideal life. So, naturally, I had to go and ruin it with the Internet.

After a couple of months of idle surfing, I came across a site called *Dominate Tricks*. It was a safe online environment where women could control men's sexuality. At first, I was disgusted, then, I tried to be amused. For a while, I was sensitive to loud sounds. Eventually, I was fascinated. I'm sure you've seen this progression many times before.

I chose the online identity of Mistress Heidi because who didn't grow up loving the adventures of the precocious Swiss maiden in an indifferent universe? And, after a few tentative sessions, I enthusiastically ordered the pathetic worms who showed up in my dungeon to lick the spikes of my shoes, feel my lash on their naked backs and upgrade the software on my desktop. (Hey! – any order can be dominatative if you growl it snarlily enough, and, in any case, why shouldn't I get a practical benefit out of my hobby?)

Anyway, after a couple of months of online domination (my high-heeled shoes – which, admittedly, I bought for the role – had never been cleaner!), I found that my dominational behaviour was slowly creeping into my offline life. It started when my 11 year-old son Garrett, apparently feeling nostalgic for when he was six months old, got fussy at the dinner table.

"If you don't eat your split pinochle soup, I will handcuff you to the table until you do!" I barked.

Well. He looked so shocked, you would have thought that I had hooked his genitals up to the generator we keep in the back in case of a gerbil apocalypse! I would never do such a thing…without his consent, or the consent of a parent or guardian. Still, he finished every drop of the soup.

A couple of weeks later, my husband Herman and I were in bed when I playfully bit his arm. There wasn't really that much blood, but, to hear him go on about it in the emergency ward, you would have thought I had bit the limb clean off! I mean, it only took a few hours for him to get the feeling back in all of his fingers! Honestly, men these days are such wimps!

The last straw was when I replaced all of the lights in my office with torches, the blinds with dark burgundy curtains and my white lab coat with black leather with lots of spikes. Lots of spikes. I go up before a hospital disciplinary review board next week.

What's happening to me?

Dr. Jaclyn

Hey, Babe,

You know how people as diverse as Oprah, Doctor Wizard of Oz and Jose Bautista of the Toronto Blue Jays advise that if you want to change your behaviour, you just have to imagine yourself acting in a different way? Imagine really hard? Really work that imagination muscle like never before (just make sure you have liniment to rub it down afterwards so it doesn't ache for the next few days)? This is sometimes known as behaviour self-modification, although it has also frequently been called behaviour self-delusion.

But, let us not be cynical.

You have been engaging in what we could call involuntary behaviour self-modification with a double summersault tuck. The more time you spend in your online persona (and, you have been spending more and more time with it, haven't you? Sure, you have – who wouldn't want clean shoes?), the more she becomes a part of you. The more she becomes you.

Being a dominatrix is NOT for kids. My advice, therefore, is to leave your husband and children and start your own dungeon in

Dear Amritsar,

Oh, wait! I'm actually Mistress Heidi in real life; I play bondage scenarios for clients in my basement. Online, I give advice on family and relationships under the name of Doctor Jackie.

I'm sorry. I...I sometimes get confused. This doesn't change anything, does it?

Heidi

Hey, Babe,

Now, you're just messing with MY head, aren't you?

Send your relationship problems to the Alternate Reality News Service's sex, love and technology columnist at questions@lespagesauxfolles.ca. Amritsar Al-Falloudjianapour is not a trained therapist, but she does know a lot of stuff. AMRITSAR SAYS: those mild electric shocks aren't your computer trying to keep you away from Web sites you shouldn't be accessing – they're your keyboard malfunctioning. You should probably replace it, unless the effect IS actually keeping you away from Web sites you shouldn't be accessing, in which case you should patent the effect and see if Microsoft would be interested in buying you out. Oh, and stock up on small bandages.

Ask Amritsar About The Tech Answer Guy

Dear Amritsar,

For Valentine's Day, my parents got my brother the video game *Deathdealer VIII: The Bottom of the Deck*. That's the one where, to finish a fight, you stick your hand down your opponent's throat, pull out his spine and, with a pair of your victim's tibias, play it like a xylophone. I, on the other hand, got the *Pinky Pinkerton in Pinktown* video game. What? You've never heard of *Pinky Pinkerton in Pinktown*? Shocker! It's a game where you get to dress up one of six female characters in over 1,000 different outfits, **all of them pink!** I mean, I'm practically an adult – I'm almost seven – and this is the kind of Valentine's Day gift my parents get me?

Oh, Amritsar! When will there be cool games for girls to play?

Jessica Wabbit

Hey, Babe,

Life sucks, and then you're buried in something pink.

Let's be honest: the <u>digital</u> game industry (video is your grandparents medium) is dominated by teenage boys or men who wish they were still teenage boys – sort of like the bar scene in Seattle. But, uhh, that's beside the point. The point is that it should surprise no one that the games they create are geared towards the interests of this very small, but very lucrative market.

Oh, and, I wouldn't consider the ultraviolent games in the *Deathdealer* series "cool." Not unless you think the events depicted in the novel *Lord of the Flies* are "cool." The whole thrust of human evolution has been to tame the violent impulses inherent in man's nature. I'm not sure that the best use of this amazing technology is to pander to the barbaric violence that lies at the heart of every man's –

Yo, Amritsar,

Tech Answer Guy here. If I may interject, I think your take on masculinity is too –

The Tech Answer Guy

Hey, Babe,

No, Tech Answer Guy, you may not interject.

Yo, Amritsar,

But, I was going to quote science at you! I was going to be all well-reasoned and intellectual! You see, in evolutionary terms, what has come to be considered masculine behaviour was –

The Tech Answer Guy

Hey, Babe,

You've got your own space where you can quote Darwin at readers. Please, do not clog up mine.

Yo, Amritsar,

Come on, baby, you know how it works. There's a three week lead time between when a column is written and when it appears in print. By the time I could respond to you in my own column, you would already have moved on to how to coordinate your bra and shoe size, or some shit like that. I didn't wanna –

The Tech Answer Guy

Hey, Babe,

Brenda! The Tech Answer Guy is intruding on my column again!

Yo Amritsar,

Aww, Jesus Begesus, do we really have to get the Editrix of the *Alternate Reality News Service* involved? Can't we settle this like Bogosian Snow Sheep?

The Tech Answer Guy

[BRENDA BRUNDTLAND-GOVANNI: Again? Seriously, you two, why can't you get along like adult advice columnists? Jesus Begesus, the two of you are lucky that my slapping gloves are out at the cleaners!]

Dear Amritsar,

So, about my question…?

Jessica Wabbit

[BRENDA BRUNDTLAND-GOVANNI: Nice shoes little girl. Did you choose them yourself, or did you go shopping with Frankenstein's monster? Tech Answer Guy! This had better be the last time you interrupt one of Amritsar's columns, or, so help me, I'll move your desk next to the Bogosian Snow Sheep pen!]

Yo, Brenda Brundtlandt-Govanni,

I hear, and I obey.

The Tech Answer Guy

[BRENDA BRUNDTLAND-GOVANNI: You better. Oh, and, Amritsar, would it kill you to grow a pair and deal with The Tech Answer Guy on your own? You should play a few rounds of *Deathdealer VIII: The Bottom of the Deck* – that'll toughen you up! I recommend Jorge the Jamaican Splatterer's foot removal move. You'll have nightmares for three days, but you'll be a better person for it!]

Hey, Babe,

So, there you have it. You should feel free to play games designed specifically for boys. And, if you're lucky, you, too can grow up to be a highly successful, if borderline psychotic, transdimensional journal editor!

Now, if you don't mind, Amritsar feels the need to sit in a candle-lit room and listen to a looped tape of waves washing over Hugh Jackman until the bad thoughts go away.

Send your relationship problems to the Alternate Reality News Service's sex, love and technology columnist at questions@lespagesauxfolles.ca. Amritsar Al-Falloudjianapour is not a trained therapist, but she does know a lot of stuff. AMRITSAR SAYS: Amritsar probably shouldn't admit this in public – she should probably save it for her Farcebook fan page – but, there is something satisfying about putting your enemy's head on a pike and displaying it at the city gate. And, playing Deathdealer VIII *can be fun, too!*

3. **BOYS**

ELWOOD WAS SURPRISED TO FIND HIS BORING LIFE BECAME BEAUTIFULLY PURE WHEN VIEWED IN N DIMENSIONS...

HOME UNIVERSE GENERATOR ™

Ask The Tech Answer Guy: Are Men Obsolete?

Yo, Tech Answer Guy,

Are men obsolete? Because, you know, my Derek is ever so sweet, and I think it would just about break his heart if I gave him the news, you know?

Sincerely,
Myrtle from Manchester

Yo, Myrts,

Obsolete? Men? Wha – whatever gave you that idea?

The Tech Answer Guy

Yo, Tech Answer Guy,

Only there was this man on the telly the other afternoon, right? And, he were saying all about how women are becoming more powerful and don't really need men any more. That's where I got the idea that men were obsolete. So, are they? I got three sons – how am I supposed to tell them summit like that?

Sincerely,
Myrtle from Manchester

Yo, Myr,

Of course, men aren't obsolete! We're young and vital and…and…and we have good teeth!

Women need men to…to have children! Of course, a lot of women don't want to have children…and, anyway, with advances in artificial insemination and cloning, it's only a matter of time before they can have children on their own…but…but, they need men to pleasure them in bed…even though most women get more pleasure from vibrators and other artificial stimulators…but – aha! A bloody ha! – vibrators won't cuddle you afterwards.

Okay, granted a lot of men won't cuddle you afterwards, either. But, those who do…will get competition from the Cuddletastic 1550. Damn research into androids with servo-mechanisms that can mimic human physical intimacy! Unlike a man, they never have to leave your side to go to the bathroom! Damn it, I say!

Umm…women need men to…to…to change flat tires. Yeah, that's it. You're driving along the highway, on your own, without a man, because you think you don't need a man any more, and – BAM! – your tire gets punctured by a stray eagle talon on the road (but not the talon of a Bald Eagle, because they're an endangered species). Then, what do you do? Eh? Eh? What do you do then?

Well, okay, you probably wait for the self-repairing nanofibres in the tire to repair the puncture and carefully drive to the next gas station where you refill the tire with air. Damn research into self-repairing nanofibres! Damn it, I say!

Still, women need men to…to…to…to kill spiders for them. Because killing insects is icky, but men seem to enjoy it. Of course, you could just get out your spidermonica and play such a sad tune on it that the spider would hang itself from its own web. Or, if you are a more compassionate sort, you could play a tune on the instrument that would make the spider pine for the freedom of an outdoor life, leading it to voluntarily leave your house.

Damn research into melodic insect control, which allows women to be their own pied spiderpipers! Damn it, I say!

Okay, but we still haven't considered – well, no, there's a good reason we haven't considered that. On the other hand – no, that makes no sense in seven states and Omaha. Still, maybe we should – no, I'm blushing just thinking about it!

Oh! Oh! Oh! Women need men to…to…to…to…to help keep the culture diverse because men think differently than women. If there are no men, who will justify giving tax breaks to the wealthy while cutting services for the poor? Okay, bad example. But, without men, who will argue in favour of pointless wars of aggression? No, that's not really convincing, either, is it? But, uhh, without men, **who will support the National Football League**?

Wow. I talked myself out of that one without even having to refer to artificial intelligence research!

Okay, you know, maybe I can't think of a reason why women need men. But, that doesn't mean that such reasons don't exist. Yeah. Sure, they do. And, I'm sure that some day, some clever social science researcher – or, maybe, a semiotic confectionary artist – will come up with it!

The Tech Answer Guy

Yo, Tech Answer Guy,

So, obsolescence it is, then? That wasn't very helpful.

Sincerely,
Myrtle from Manchester

Yo, Myr,

No! Wait! I've got it! Women need men to have somebody to feel superior to, somebody that they can pat on the head when things go wrong – as things inevitably will for us – and coo, "Oh, that's too bad," to while secretly feeling that warm glow of "I'm so glad I'm not you!"

Is that fair? Well…men have felt superior to women for thousands of years, so I guess it was your turn. Be gentle.

If you are a dude with a question about the latest technology, ask The Tech Answer Guy by sending it to questions@lespagesauxfolles.ca. Just remember: there IS an "us" in penis. If you say the word the right way…

Ask The Tech Answer Guy About the Meat of the Matter

Yo, Tech Answer Guy,

For a number of years, now, I have been having these vivid nightmares about Steve McGarrett chasing down a serial killer: cholesterol. Towards the – the number, by the way, was 17. Towards the end of the dream, he corners the killer and gives the classic line: "eBook 'em, Danno." But, they get the wrong waxy steroid of fat! They arrest the good kind of cholesterol instead of the evil kind!

Ever since the dreams started, I have been…hesitant to barbecue red meat.

There was the time a couple of years back when I was forced to take over for my older brother, Trony (the n is silent), who had come down with a nasty case of roof rot just as the burgers needed to be flipped on the grill. The ensuing – a couple meaning seven. The ensuing events have come to be known throughout the family as "the chipotle incident." Although everybody ultimately survived (although some would never be able to simultaneously walk and listen to the Beach Boys again) and all the charges were dropped, my problem with barbecuing was laid bare for everybody in the family to see. It was years – five – before I could show my face at another family gathering.

I was seriously considering turning in my tongs and "kiss the stupid, chef" apron when I read about this meat that was grown in vats – no actual cows were involved! The meat was created with extra vitamins **and low cholesterol!** Could it be true? Was artificial lab meat the solution to my barbecuing abashedness?

I had to break into Grummeau-Ceti Labs, the research wing of The Future Lies in Plastics, LLC, to find out because there were no plans to market the meat to the public. And, as I stood there with the test tube steak in my hands, alarm bells going off around me, I knew I had found the solution to my red meat timidity. I knew then and there that I could look the son I never had straight up the nose and say, "Come on, kid. We got us some barbecuing to do!"

This just leaves me with one problem. Should I cook the vat grown steaks with Hunt's Bold BBQ sauce, or go straight for the Bull's Eye Grilled Onion and Garlic Showdown?

Sincerely,
Troy from Troy

Yo, Troy,

That's saccri – saccharine – no, sacred legs – sacre...bleu – sacre bleu, that's sacrilege! Not only that, but it's just wrong!

Our ancestors used to slaughter living animals and smear themselves with the animal's blood before roasting the gutted carcasses over an open fire. Okay, we've come a long way since then, and I recognize that Sunday afternoon football isn't really a compensation for not smearing ourselves with the blood of our kill. Still, smearing yourself with agar from a Petri dish is even further away from our hunter/gatherer ancestors!

Let me put it this way: lab grown steaks taste of scientific hubris, and that's not something that can be masked with even the strongest barbecue sauce!

Still not convinced? Chew on this: the Massachusetts Institution of Technology's Digital Cuisine Programme recently conducted a blind taste test of cow-bred steak and test tube-bred steak. The result? Nine out of 10 participants wanted their sight back. When they were told that that wasn't possible, six out of the nine hated the artificial meat. So, there you go.

Besides, The Tech Answer Guy prefers Grumpy's Goodnight Loving Barbecue Sauce. Any regular reader would know that!

The Tech Answer Guy

Yo, Tech Answer Guy,

I…I don't know how to say this but…a friend of mine once offered me a piece of test tube created back bacon. I figured it would taste horrible and that would be the end of that little culinary experiment, but, instead, I liked it. I liked it a lot. Now, I've got a six rasher a day habit that I just can't break. Okay, honestly, that I don't want to break. That's right: I now prefer back bacon grown in a test tube to the real thing.

Oh, Tech Answer Guy, is there any hope for me?

Sincerely,
Troi from Troy

Yo, Troi,

You are, indeed, a lost soul. The next time I'm barbecuing out back, I shall pray for you.

The Tech Answer Guy

If you are a dude with a question about the latest technology, ask The Tech Answer Guy by sending it to questions@lespagesauxfolles.ca. Just remember: just because you can make just about anything tasty if you soak it in the right marinade and cook it on a grill doesn't mean that you should. Especially when I'm not invited.

Ask The Tech Answer Guy About Industrial Lubricants

Yo, Tech Answer Guy,

I work the line at the Nakamichi Flesh Companion plant in Indianapolis, Sri Lanka. You could say I'm a tits and ass man. That's not a personal fetish – I inspect the breasts and butts as they come off the assembly line to ensure they meet the company's exacting standards for female pulchritude, as laid out in the Flesh Companion Production Code, v. 7.283e. (My personal fetish is for the third finger of a woman's right hand – my friends tell me that's weird, but you probably get it a lot. Right? RIGHT? Yeah. Sure. Of course, you do…)

I worked the line for thirty years; I can honestly say that I have seen more female flesh than the security detail at Hef's mansion! And, all that time, I was carefully saving every penny I could. Finally, with an employee discount and a student loan (well, it would prove to be a learning experience, wouldn't it?), I was able to purchase one of Nakamichi's Flesh Companions for myself.

I called her Irma Ge.

Irma Ge was a low-end model, with a small body, no attachments and a lack of knowledge of international literature. But, she came fully programmed with Julia Child, Mata Hari and Tera Patrick sub-routines, so I would just have to live without discussions of Haruki Murakami's latest novel.

At first, Irma Ge's presence in my life made all the sacrifice worthwhile. I mean, we screwed like virtual rabbits! She also made a mean three bean quail lasagna. Unfortunately, about three months into the relationship, I got a rash on my…umm…private parts.

At first, I did what any self-respecting man would do: I ignored the rash in the hope that it would go away. Unfortunately, our continued virtual rabbiting activity made the rash worse in ways that my lawyer tells me the contract with the company forbids me from making public. What I can say is that the doctor I was eventually forced – against everything the Macho Code of Manliness stands for – to see informed me that I have a skin sensitivity to Neoprene 47, the lubricant Irma Ge uses for all of her joints and, err, various other body parts.

I could try to substitute a different lubricant for the one she uses, but that would probably void the warranty. Then, if Irma Ge decided to do something crazy like serve me squid with lug nut sauce or become a Maoist and start demanding the overthrow of the IMF or explain how the different levels of reality interact in *1Q84* I would not be able to ask the company to help stop her. On the other hand, the contract clearly states that I am not entitled to a refund or an exchange.

Is there anything I can do?

Sincerely,
Zaphod of Beeblebrox Juice

Yo, Albert,

First off, I gotta thank your lawyer for advising you not to share with the rest of us the details of how your rash spread. Some people read The Tech Answer Guy with their morning breakfast, you know.

As for your little problem, did you ever watch the *Twilight Zone*? And, I'm not talking about the first revival in the 1980s, or the second revival in 2002, or – heaven forfend! – the 1983 film! No, I'm talking about the original series from the 1950s. You know, the one where William Shatner played the guy who saw a demon on the wing of his plane, but couldn't get anybody else to believe him? Man, was that creepy!

Umm. Yeah. Anyhow. Most of the shows ended with an ironic twist not unlike the one you describe. Then, they would fade to black and you would have to wait a week for another episode. Your story sounded like it would make a good episode of the *Twilight Zone*. A not safe for work, lock up your daughters, "What's your problem with women, buste – err, oh, ick, on second thought, don't tell me" episode of the *Twilight Zone*. Still.

So, my suggestion to you would be to either find a magnifying glass so that you can read all of the books in the library you now have time for, or accept the limp as the price you pay for the wisdom gained from the experience of reliving your youth.

Oh, and, private parts? Really? Do you know how many people read The Tech Answer Guy?

The Tech Answer Guy

If you are a dude with a question about the latest technology, ask The Tech Answer Guy by sending it to questions@lespagesauxfolles.ca. Just remember: references to classic science fiction shows aren't always as insightful as you might think they would be.

Ask The Tech Answer Guy: A Really Bad Day

Yo, Tech Answer Guy,

Does a man cave have to be in an actual cave?

Sincerely,
Johann Gambolputty-de-von-Ausfern-schplenden-schlitter-crass-cren-bon-fried-digger-dingle-dangle-dongle-dungle-burstein-von-knacker-thrasher-apple-banger-horowitz-ticolensic-grander-knotty-spelltinkle-grandlich-grumblemeyer-spelter-wasser-kurstlich-himble-eisen-bahnwagen-guten-abend-bitte-ein-nürnburger-bratwürstel-gespurten-mitz-weimache-luber-hundsfut-gumberaber-schönendanker-kalbsfleisch-mittleraucher-von-Hautkopft from Ulm

Yo, Johann…Gambolputty-de-von-Ausfern-schplenden-schlitter-crass-cren-bon-fried-digger-dingle-dangle-dongle-dungle-burstein-von-knacker-thrasher-apple-banger-horowitz-ticolensic-grander-knotty-spelltinkle-grandlich-grumblemeyer-spelter-wasser-kurstlich-himble-eisen-bahnwagen-guten-abend-bitte-ein-nürnburger-bratwürstel-gespurten-mitz-weimache-luber-hundsfut-gumberaber-schönendanker-kalbsfleisch-mittleraucher-von-Hautkopft,

Yes. Yes, it does.

The Tech Answer Guy

Yo, Tech Answer Guy,

Really? Because, you know, I thought the term "man cave" was just a metaphor for a room in a house where a man could establish his dominance by surrounding himself with manly things. You know, like, huge beer steins (on doilies, of course, so you don't leave stains on the furniture) and the crutches your favourite football player used that month he was out of the lineup with an ingrown fungal infection on his right big toe and – dammit – forget the doilies, because this is a man cave and if a man wants to leave rings on the furniture, then – dammit a second time, dammit I say (even a third time) – that's his right as a man.
　　Right?

Sincerely,
Everybody Just Calls Me Larry from Ulm

Yo, Everybody Just Calls Me Larry,

Thanks for simplifying the name thing.
　　As for your question – if I can presume to pick it out of that dense thicket of a paragraph – real men don't do metaphors. Metaphors just get in the way of direct communication. If it were more socially acceptable, real men would communicate entirely with grunts and hand gestures.

We only use language to get by in the world, only to the absolute minimum necessary to get our point across, and never metaphorically.

So, when I use the term man cave, I am actually talking about a room carved out of solid rock, preferably high on a cliff face. Our ancestors used to live in caves, and if holes in solid rock were good enough for them – I would say dammit, but Mrs. The Tech Answer Guy is trying to teach me couth – they're good enough for real men. If you don't believe me, just ask your grandfather.

The Tech Answer Guy

Yo, Tech Answer Guy,

You make a good point, and I would hate to argue with you, you being The Tech Answer Guy and all, but wouldn't it be difficult to get electricity into a room carved out of solid rock high on a cliff face? And, if you couldn't get electricity up there, how would you be able to light the cave so you could watch your 40 inch, 3D, 4F, hi-5, 6-of-one TV? Studies have conclusively shown that watching television in the dark dramatically increases your risk of hearing loss.

Sincerely,
Larry from Ulm

Yo, Lar from Ul,

Yeah, yeah. On the one hand, real men enjoy their fictional drama, and what's a little hearing loss when there's a new episode of *Once Upon a Time* to be watched? On the other hand, are you serious?

I asked my grandfather, Granpa The Tech Answer Guy, your question. He told me that, a long time ago, in the Plasticine Era, men would rub two sticks together until they ignited, then use the burning stick to set a carefully configured group of branches ablaze. And, if that didn't work, they'd use a Zippo. This fire would allow them to watch TV all night, and, of course, they would have no trouble watching in the day as long as their cave faced west towards the sunrise.

I have to say, though, that I am sensing some resistance on your part to the traditional conception of the man cave.

The Tech Answer Guy

Yo, Tech Answer Guy,

Well, yeah, okay, sure, that makes sense, I guess. Still, there seem to be other problems with your conceptualization of the man cave. For instance: how would it be possible to get a Wi-Fi signal through solid rock? I'm a popular guy – how am I supposed to survive in a man cave if I can't check my email every 30 seconds?

Sincerely,
L. from U.

Yo, L.,

Have you ever heard of smoke signals? Believe me, if you make a fire in your man cave, you will be generating a lot of smoke – learn how to harness that for your communication.

Okay, we are clearly beyond resistance here and into open defiance. Sorry, but I cannot allow that to continue. L., if that is your real name, the Tech Answer Guy is cutting you off. No more questions until you can prove to me that you adhere to the Macho Code of Manliness!

The Tech Answer Guy

If you are a dude with a question about the latest technology, ask The Tech Answer Guy by sending it to questions@lespagesauxfolles.ca. Just remember: a core meltdown of your computer, causing you to lose all of your data, can sour even the most die-hard tech-head on new technology. I'm just sayin'...

Ask Amritsar About
The Health Aspects of an Unusual Diet

Dear Amritsar,

Our 15 year-old son Timmy is a little green around the edges and doesn't pick up his feet when he walks, but, despite being a zombie, is a good kid who gets decent grades at school and relates well to his siblings, who do not share his...affliction. I am, however, a little worried about his diet.

Whenever I try to encourage him to eat more vegetables, he just stares at me and moans, "Braaaaaains!" I've begged him to eat high fibre cereals for breakfast, but he just stares at me and moans, "Braaaaaains!" I don't know how many times I have asked him to take vitamin supplements to make up for the nutrients he is missing, but he just stares at me and moans, "Braaaaaains!"

Should I worry about Timmy's...unusual diet? And, if so, is there anything I can do to change it?

June Cleaver

Hey, Babe,

The teen years are difficult enough for most children, but they are especially hard on zombies.

Vampires are the cool kids in the schoolyard. Werewolves are the jocks. Ghosts are the artsy types. Recombined and reanimated children are the class clowns (albeit, not always intentionally). Zombies? Well, let's be honest, zombies are the chess nerds of the supernatural high school set, the one clique that all the others look down upon.

You are right to be concerned about Timmy's diet. Without the proper vitamins, his bones will become brittle and his limbs will become prone to breaking off…well, more prone to breaking off than they already are. I do not want to alarm you, but that's the least of his problems: without a proper balance of fruit and meat, your son's brain will shrivel and become increasingly dysfunctional, which will likely make it difficult for him to get into a good college (unless he was planning on going into law).

Some experts in the field of Neo-Thanatical Nutrition Studies have suggested that this is just a phase your son is going through, and that he will probably outgrow it if he doesn't get shot in the head before his 20th birthday. However, most research indicates that, if not short-circuited early, the hunger for braaaaaains among undead children will follow them for the rest of their lives.

Trying to reason with your child will likely prove futile, for obvious reasons. You might want to consider cognitive therapy to counter Timmy's obsessive eating behaviours. Unfortunately, tests conducted at the New England School of Zombie Apocalypse Medicine indicate that four out of five researchers are murdered within minutes of beginning clinical trials, while the fifth researcher ends up in a desolate building in the woods with a disparate band of strangers fighting for their survival. At best, I would consider these tests to be inconclusive.

Some parents resort to trickery to get their zombie children to eat a healthier diet. You could, for instance, try to cook high fibre muffins using molds in the shape of braaaaaains (which can be conveniently purchased for 99 cents at the Dollar Store, if not stolen from a neighbour who appears to have vanished). Some parents have taken to mashing vitamins into a fine powder and mixing them into their zombie children's breakfast braaaaaains, which, while disgusting, does tend to go unnoticed by the child.

While subterfuges like these may seem like an acceptable short term solution, they don't address the main problem: your child's insistence on eating unhealthily. Your reluctance to confront your child when it is trying to get its hands around your throat so that it can chomp on your head (the ellipses in your question may have given away more of your fears than you realize) is understandable, but you have to put aside your personal insecurities and do what is best for little Timmy.

Nobody said being a parent was easy. Especially during a zombie apocalypse.

Send your relationship problems to the Alternate Reality News Service's *sex, love and technology columnist at questions@lespagesauxfolles.ca. Amritsar Al-Falloudjianapour is not a trained therapist, but she does know a lot of stuff. AMRITSAR SAYS: even though emotions on the subject of the depiction of women in computer games run high, there is no excuse for tweeting something like: "evil femiNazi hos should suk my dik & die!" You should, instead, write: "I would appreciate it if evil femiNazi prostitutes would suck my dick and die!" High emotions are no excuse for poor spelling or general incivility!*

Ask The Tech Answer Guy About Winning the Argument

Yo, Tech Answer Guy,

I have been having an ongoing debate with Gorgias the Sophist. He is apparently of the belief that Non-being is an image. Pfft to that, I say. Absolutely pfft! To my mind, the Other is Non-being by another name, and it turns out to be the case, not only that the Other is, but that Being and beings participate in it and hence in some sense are not.

This argument feels like it has been going on for eons. Is there any way I can use Twitter to end it definitively?

Sincerely,
Plato from Athens

Yo, Plats,

It's hard to argue Being and Nothingness in 140 characters or less. Nietzsche tried it and ended up in a madhouse. Wittgenstein managed to pull it off, but that's only because nobody ever understood what he was going on about regardless of the length. Descartes managed to write one memorable Tweet, but then he ruined it by following up with a 500 page treatise.

The problem with Twitter is, of course, that just when you start to grapple with an issue, when you're really wrestling with an idea, really throwing it to the ground and doing your best to pin its squirming form down, you run out of space. Consider, for example, this argument from your own work:

```
And, at first he would most easily discern
the shadows and, after that, the
likenesses or reflections in water of men
and other things, and
```

And, what? Then, he would go have a sandwich and contemplate the perfect ratio of cheese to meat? Or, would he throw himself in the water in an attempt to embrace the reflections of men, only to explain that he really needed to bathe after a long day's think when those around him laughed? Or, would he simply give up the whole philosophical enterprise and work at his father's toga factory?

Twitter is hell on philosophers.

You might consider serial tweets. This worked for Sophocles, although some would argue that Oedipus the King is a more compelling character than Gorgias the Sourpuss. Still, if you did that, your next tweet would be:

```
later, the things themselves, and from
these he would go on to contemplate the
appearances in the heavens and heaven
itself, more easily by
```

Gods, you really know how to create dramatic tension, don't you? More easily by...what, exactly? By stomping on the foot of a Guardian, thereby ensuring swift passage to the afterlife? By cleaning the pig excrement off his sandals? By watching *Buckwild* on his 27 inch high definition television, an anachronism that would cause the entire edifice of rational Greek thought to implode?

The problem with serial tweets is that they are subject to the law of diminishing returns (as any clerk in a shop in the agora will know from the day after a major festival). By the fourth tweet, your followers will be wondering if you've been lecturing in the sun too long. By the eleventh tweet, they will be considering unfollowing you and wondering if perhaps Merenptah has been tweeting the latest LOLBasts.

If you really want to be effective, you need to use Twitter for what it does best: ridiculing your philosophical opponents. And, although he may not have advanced degrees in Smart Shit, that is something The Tech Answer Guy can help you with! Why don't you try something like:

```
yo, Gorgias the Sophist - yo Momma's so
fat, she could hold the entire Senate in
her mouth and still eat a roast boar!
```

Or,

```
yo, Gorgias the Sophist - if perception is
reality, I perceive that you sleep with
Menarchis' sheep!
```

Or,

```
yo, Gorgias the Sophist - you have my
whole fallacy wrong!
```

Engaging in this manner of discourse may seem beneath a philosopher of your stature. Get over it, Curdled Olive Oil Breath!

The Tech Answer Guy

If you are a dude with a question about the latest technology, ask The Tech Answer Guy by sending it to questions@lespagesauxfolles.ca. Just remember: shouting "what you are saying is totally spacious!" will not win you an argument. Are you suggesting that it has enough leg room to comfortably seat a family of four? Or, perhaps, that it belongs to Kevin Spacey? Why would Kevin Spacey's involvement invalidate an argument? He seems like an intelligent enough fellow (his appearance in Fred Claus *notwithstanding). Granted, this may just be a translation problem; ancient Greek is slippier than a greased eel in a vat of refried coconut butter. However, I believe the term you actually should have used was "speciesist."*

Ask The Tech Answer Guy: Tell it to the Hand!

Yo, Tech Answer Guy,

The other day, I was slapped in the face for no apparent reason by a woman at my local MultiMaxiMegaMart. I was standing in the 3.14 items or less line; I was there to buy bottled washers and, for some reason, had a Luxury sized box of weasel chow in my cart. It made no sense: my weasel only eats Captain Clench cereal. Damn the store's seductive layout! In any case, the woman insisted that I was fondling her frozen foods, even though I was not aware of doing any such thing.

I would have denied it, but it wasn't the first time this had happened.

A couple of weeks ago, I was standing in line to get into Blargh Blargh's, an exclusive club run by Venusian Blurt Splunk, when I was slapped by a woman standing in front of me. She claimed that I had been inappropriately groping her in the spandex. I didn't even know that that was part of a woman's anatomy!

Then, 10 days later, which would have made it...umm...carry the 12...subtract the square root of obliviousness...assassinate the crown prince of Prussia...four days ago, I was called into the office of my boss at Durston Dunst Detweiller Prokofiev, who said that I had been accused of sexual harassment. Apparently, three of the interns claimed that in the last five months I had groped them in the photocopying room. Since we work in a paperless office, I assumed that was a euphemism for a part of their anatomy. This may not have gone anywhere – they were only interns, after all – if I hadn't been caught on videotape in front of 27 witnesses at a retirement party! Even so, I had no conscious recollection that I had been doing it!

Is there any explanation for this behaviour? Any explanation at all?

Sincerely,
Samar from Samarkand

Yo, Sammy,

Do you mean an explanation that doesn't make you look like a miserable, woman-hating sexist scumbag?

The Tech Answer Guy

Yo, Tech Answer Guy,

Well, yeah.

Sincerely,
Samar from Samarkand

Yo, Sammy,

Okay, then. Because according to the Macho Code of Manliness, being a miserable, woman-hating sexist scumbag is not cool. Not cool at all.

So, assuming that you are, as you say, not a miserable, woman-hating sexist scumbag, I can tell you that, according to *Technological Neuropathy for Dummies*, you have Kinext Konsciousness. This is similar to Krishna Konsciousness, but with better graphics. Oh, and except for the fact that they are actually nothing alike.

Kinext Konsciousness is what happens when you spend too much time playing computer games that use a physical interface. You start to develop a – nervous may be overstating the case a bit, so let's call it mildly concerned – you start to develop a mildly concerned physical tic, one that is neither conscious nor controllable.

Hardcore players often find their bodies doing things without their knowledge. For example, after a three day *Wayne Gretzky Tennis* binge, Arthur California of New York City randomly slapped customers at the *Shemp's Shoes* where he worked. For another example, assembly line worker Charlie Nuevos-Yorke of Los Angeles made wrench turning motions whenever he walked past anything resembling the head of a screw. For a third example – what? Two examples aren't good enough for you? You know, when I started out in this racquet, one example and a Bronx cheer was all that a columnist felt responsible to give his readers. Be thankful we've evolved since then!

Some neuroscientists believe that there is no such thing as Kinext Konsciousness, that it's just an excuse for men to engage in anti-social behaviour without consequence. They point out that no women have ever been diagnosed with the condition, which, okay, yeah, The Tech Answer Guy will admit does look a little, you know, *gershlumptfen*. They also say that experiments have shown that, other than an increase in potato chip consumption and a decrease in tolerance for Honey Boo Boo, lab rats are not affected by playing 1,000 straight hours of *Star Blap: Assault on the Death Store* on the Kinext.

You'd better hope that this is just because women's physignomy – pissiognomy – physimoggy – oh, you know: body structure! – is different from men's, and that the lab experiments didn't factor in the weight of the hydrogen atom divided by the laundry load and crucial factor of colours or whites. Otherwise, that would make you a miserable, woman-hating sexist scumbag. And, that wouldn't be cool.

The Tech Answer Guy

If you are a dude with a question about the latest technology, ask The Tech Answer Guy by sending it to questions@lespagesauxfolles.ca. Just remember: human sexuality is a beautiful thing, especially when it involves the latest polystyrene synthetic skin and 247 pre-programmed settings/positions!

Ask Amritsar About Poll Dancing

Dear Amritsar,

I'm sexy. But, don't just take my word for it. In 2009, I topped *Peephole Magazine*'s Sexiest Man Ever! (This Year) readers' poll. I won MCTV5's Sexy! Sexier! Sexiest! Man poll in the same year. Then, I won an Oscar for Sexiest Man in a Leading Role in a Comedy, Musical or Puppet Film. In fact, I have won 57 sexiest man in the world polls in the last five years. Hey! – I feel another one coming on even as we speak!

However, no matter how much I smolder, smirk or...something else that begins with the letter combination "sm," I cannot seem to win a Golden Wombat Sexiest Man Alive poll in either the Scented or Non-scented category. Why not? Never mind – I don't need to know. What I really want to know is: what can I do to win?

Ryan R.

Hey, Babe,

You know I would be willing to give up the advice column writing racket to have your children, but, honestly, *Green Lantern*? WTF!?!

As to your little problem, you seem to be a victim of the corporate consolidation of organizations that conduct online sexiness polls. In 2007, Golden Gumbo Productions, which makes the Golden Wombat line of products that includes Golden Wombat body spray, Golden Wombat hair gel and Golden Wombat scented bath oil spritzer, was bought out by Mensa, the smarty-pants group.

Their second move after the takeover was to restrict voting on the Sexiest Man and Sexiest Woman Alive poll to anybody with an IQ of 140 or more. (Their first move was to replace celebrity spokesmodels with mathematical equations with seven or more variables.) Needless to say, that has radically changed who has won the poll (not to mention how teenagers view their body care products).

Last year's Sexiest Man Alive was 67 year-old particle physicist Bernie Ploitkin of the Walk the Max Planck Institute.

The previous year's winner, Meldrum Hashtag, has long been touted as a shoe-in for a Nobel Prize in Mathematics, which is ironic considering that advanced arthritis of the shins makes it impossible for him to comfortably wear shoes. The Sexiest Man Alive the year before that was the large hadron collider. This was odd because, of course, at the time the poll was taken, it wouldn't come online for another 18 months – clearly, the write-in vote carried the day.

Marilyn vos Savant has been the sexiest woman alive as far back as anybody can remember.

Look. Perceived sexiosity is a very personal thing. One woman's sexy beast is another woman's Prometheus Society reject. You might want to accept that this one poll is not for you. I'm sure crying into your 57 (and counting) other Sexiest Man Alive polls will be of much comfort to you.

Dear Amritsar,

So, I should maybe read some books or something?

Ryan R.

Hey, Babe,

Siiiiiiigh!

Dear Amritsar,

Last year, I won the Golden Gumbo Sexiest Man Alive poll. Me! With my bad back and glasses with lenses so thick you could use them to fry an anthill…on another continent! I'm not kidding: the FBI has asked me to register my glasses as weapons of mass destruction! If they were any heavier, I would need a tractor-trailer to wear them! Let's just say that if I had been in *Goldfinger*, James Bond's genitalia would not have gotten away in one piece!

This was the first time I had won anything like it! It's better than the MacArthur Fellowship (although MacArthur groupies are awesome, I must say)! It's waaaaay better than an honorary doctorate (as it happens, I only have 17) , and moderately to somewhat heavily better than an actual doctorate (three).

I love this feeling! How can I win more Sexiest Man Alive polls?

Bernie P.

Hey, Babe,

Is nobody happy with who they are any more? Nobody?

Send your relationship problems to the Alternate Reality News Service's *sex, love and technology columnist at questions@lespagesauxfolles.ca.   Amritsar   Al-Falloudjianapour is not a trained therapist, but she does know a lot of stuff. AMRITSAR SAYS: you know when you're at an orgy and you're tempted to break out your PDA and work on a spreadsheet because the deadline on your current project looms large and your career hangs in the balance and you won't be able to keep your high-maintenance spouse without it, so you have a porn video ready at the touch of a button in case anybody asks what you're looking at so you can tell them, "A dirty movie. You know, to help get me in the mood?" DON'T DO THAT! It's tacky.*

Ask The Tech Answer Guy the Hard Question

Yo, Tech Answer Guy,

I was recently diagnosed as suffering from ED (not to be confused with my second wife, Edie, which was a whole different kind of suffering!). At 78, I felt I didn't have the time to wait for traditional cures to prove their efficacy, so I went to a clinic in the heart of the deepest wilds of uncivilized London to try an unproven experimental treatment that promised immediate results.

The basic idea, as I understand it, was to implant electrodes into my brain and small motors into my penis. Then, as I barely understand it but am bulling my way through the explanation in any case, all I had to do was think of sex and I could will myself to have an erection. As I don't understand it at all, a wireless doohickey transferred the firings of my cerebral whatsis to the servo…somethings in my penis. Or, something like that.

At first, it was splendiferous. Whenever I just thought of Editta, my fifth wife, I got a bear down there. That first night, we made love for over three minutes – a new record! I could probably have gone longer, but my heart monitor sounded like a four alarm fire, and it spooked the horses.

This would have been the end of the story, except I started getting hard ons outside of the bedroom. Women showing cleavage. Women wearing surgical stockings. Women breathing – the slightest thing would set it off. When I was in public, my erection would sometimes go for hours without surcease. That's not as much fun as it sounds. In fact – ouch!

The doctors are afraid that removing the apparatus would be bad for my health. Can you recommend anything that might alleviate my distress?

Sincerely,
The Donnie from None of Your Business

Yo, Don,

You lucky dog! We should all be so fortunate as to have enough of a fortune to enable us to get a highly iffy medical intervention that will allow us to get an eRection whenever we want! eRection – get it? Ha ha ha! Can you imagine a couple getting this done for their 50th wedding anniversary and finding whole new ways to pleasure each other? Disgusting to think about, and yet oddly hopeful, as well.

The Tech Answer Guy

Yo, Tech Answer Guy,

No, no, you don't understand. I can't leave my house without getting an…alright, an eRection. And, now, even staying inside isn't helping. I got an eRection the other day looking at a news report on nuclear energy because the tops of the reactors reminded me of women's breasts! I got hard playing with my toy train set when the engine approached a tunnel – and I don't even know who this Sigmund Freud chappie is!

Can you please help me find a way to put an end to this?

Sincerely,
The Donnie from None of Your Business

Yo, Dons,

Oh, yeah, I can see that <snigger>this situation must be really hard for you</snigger>.

The Tech Answer Guy

Yo, Tech Answer Guy,

This isn't a joke, you simpering blaggard! I get hard when I look at a crack in the pavement! I'm hard right now, and I'm just banging the keys on my keyboard! Heeeeeeeelp meeeeeeeeee!

Sincerely,
The Donnie from None of Your Business

Yo, Don-Man,

Lighten up! Yes, I'm sure that eRections have their drawbacks. Still, think of all the millions of men out there in the world who, through no fault of their own – or, at worst, 49% of their own fault, which is not a majority, so they can at least be considered statistically blameless – cannot raise the flag, as it were. Don't you think they would envy your ability to get hard on demand?

If you can't be happy for yourself, be grateful you're not one of them!

The Tech Answer Guy

Yo, Tech Answer Guy,

This is to inform you that The Donnie from None of Your Business recently underwent a successful lobotomy and is no longer able to keep up his correspondence with you. Thank you for your interest in The Donnie from None of Your Business, and the best of luck with your future endeavours.

Sincerely,
Bert Toadst, Legal Council
The Donnie from None of Your Business

Yo, Bertster,

It's probably for the best. Dude had no idea how lucky he was.

The Tech Answer Guy

PS: <snigger>"Keep up" his correspondence!</snigger>

If you are a dude with a question about the latest technology, ask The Tech Answer Guy by sending it to questions@lespagesauxfolles.ca. Just remember: the quality of The Tech Answer Guy's advice is usually inversely proportional to the entertainment value your question gives him.

Ask The Tech Answer Guy: Intelligence Is Annoying

Yo, Tech Answer Guy,

A couple of months ago, I bought a Smart Model Tfortwo car. It was a steal at 150 Greek Euros. And, when I say steal, I mean the owner insisted that I ask him no questions about it.

I'm not a one to look a gift horse in the exhaust manifold (I don't usually travel with a change of shirts), so I agreed.

The guy I bought it from did mention that the car's onboard artificial intelligence had an MA in Existential Philosophy, but I thought nothing of it at the time. I thought he meant the AI had studied the existence of tents.

I was almost immediately proven wrong, when, driving the car home, I asked it if Avington Avenue would be a shortcut. "Avington Avenue has no exit," the car informed me. "But, then, we all ultimately have No Exit…"

Ooooo-kaaaaay. No problem. I could take my normal route.

A couple of days later, on an errand to get my girlfriend a bottle of kippered hams, I asked the car for the shortest route to the Swelldon Market. "You could take the Exegesis Expressway to Kings Road, travel for five metres and turn off on Pauper's Lane, but, then, all roads lead to the same place in the end, don't they?"

As I set out to find the Exegesis Expressway, I asked the car what it meant by that last bit, but all it told me was: "If all roads lead to the same place, shortcuts are really beside the point, wouldn't you say?" As a matter of fact, I wouldn't say. I was already 20 minutes late.

My car was making me think. I hate thinking. I'm a stock broker with a staple marriage (it's held together with…well, you get the idea…) and a collection of common *Star Blap* baseball cards (check out the stats on Jabba the Catcher – he can't hit, but he really knows how to cover the plate!). Thinking gives me the sensation of a fire being lit in my nose!

The final straw was on a trip to Swindon, when the car advised me: "Look not into the turnoff ramp to I47 lest it be that the turnoff ramp to I47 be looking into you." I was so angry at this unasked for bit of philosophy that I purposefully missed the I47, adding 20 minutes to the trip and making me late for my sister Josephina's bris.

I don't enjoy being made to feel stupid by my automobile. That's what family is for.

So, should I torch the car for the insurance money?

Sincerely,
Derf from Dusseldorf

Yo, Derf,

Absolutely. Burn the bastard. Burn it to the ground. Then, burn the ashes. After that, burn the concept of the ashes. Because, you know, there's nothing suspicious about a car in the middle of a parking lot spontaneously combusting. I'll bet you dollars to doughnuts (whatever **that** means) that not only will the police give you a medal for great public service, but your insurance company will drop your premiums on the theory that, having had one car burn down to its basic concept, the odds of that happening again to you are that much smaller!

Or, no, wait, I have a better idea! Why don't you crash the car into a tree at high speeds. (Make sure your seat belt is properly fastened and your airbags are fully functional – wouldn't want anybody to get hurt.) Then, when the cops want to know what happened, you tell them that you had to swerve off the road to avoid hitting Bambi. That's right – you totalled your car to avoid killing the loveable Disney cartoon character. That should get you a parade down Main Street!

Or – and I know this is going to sound crazy, but hear me out – you could **take the car back to the person you bought it from and ask them to disable the onboard AI!** Oh, sure, it's not as dramatic as the other scenarios, but, on the bright side, **it's not as dramatic as the other scenarios!** Life already throws enough traumas at us – remember being born? Why create more?

Besides, if your car's AI is really committed to its existentialism, it will expect you to shut it down. Hell is owners perplexed!

The Tech Answer Guy

If you are a dude with a question about the latest technology, ask The Tech Answer Guy by sending it to questions@lespagesauxfolles.ca. Just remember: according to the Macho Code of Manliness (MCM), popularity is a sign of weakness. If 300 taught us anything, it is that the true man only befriends those he is about to die next to in battle.

Ask The Tech Answer Guy About the Bloody Drinks

Yo, Tech Answer Guy,

What goes good with blood?

Sincerely,
Vlad from Tara Motilar, Transylvania

Yo, V-lad,

This is a good question. According to the Macho Code of Manliness (MCM), manly men must spend at least 37 per cent of their free time (defined as: "...time not at work but not including time spent on relationships, because, you know, waddya gonna do?") brawling in bars, tracking down serial killers at great personal cost to themselves or being gored by bulls in Pamplona (which, if memory serves, is a suburb of

Detroit). As you can imagine, getting blood on your clothes is a regular part of the experience of being a man.

I have found that a good way to offset blood stains that favour one side of a shirt is to spill wine on the other side. If you do it with enough care, you can get a red Rorschach pattern thing going. Then, when friends ask, "What the hell...?" you can respond, "What the hell does it look like?" Then, they'll go, "Oh. Umm. Well, let me ponder this for a moment..." Well moderated, the ensuing discussion can last for hours without once touching on the issue of your personal hygiene.

You may have heard that a combination of lemon oil, Worsetoshi – Worthoghire – barbecue sauce and fairy dust can get blood out of clothes. The evidence is inconclusive, but that may be beside the point: the Strategic Fairy Dust Reserves have been depleted by years of governments that insisted lowering taxes would increase government revenues, and grinding your own fairies is both backbreaking work and more than a little disgusting. Because of this, fairy dust, like justice, is only available to the very rich.

Some people, knowing that they are about to engage in activities which will result in punctured flesh (including bare-knuckled boxing, bronco busting and defending the theory of evolution in a room full of Evangelicals), will wear red clothes to conceal the blood. I cannot begin to explain why this is a bad idea that will not wor

The Tech Answer Guy

Yo, Tech Answer Guy,

Ah, no. Thank you for what some people will, I am sure, find fascinating and useful information, but, actually, that was not what I had intended to ask. Please forgive me: when you have lived for over 900 years, your communication tends to get somewhat terse.

I am having a dinner party for a few of my undead friends next week. I have several bottles of blood on ice for the occasion, but, you know, after a century or two, blood served neat starts to become a little…stale. Predictable. Not at all tasty any more. I have tried various mixers – blood and Coke was an especially disgusting concoction, and not in a good way – but none of them worked. Olives get gummy when soaked in blood, and onions become nearly impossible to peel.

So, in this context, what goes good with blood?

Sincerely,
Vlad from Tara Motilar, Transylvania

Yo, V-Lad,

Oh. Yeah. Of course. I knew that. Course I did.

I would recommend freshly extracted yak's eyes. I am told that they are delicious when soaked for 3.7 seconds in blood, and the fact that they always appear to be looking directly at the drinker will add just the right frisson of creepiness to your event.

Of course, when I say I, I mean Angus Winchester, esteemed British mixologist and used battery art curator.

I/Angus Winchester have also found that turpentine makes the perfect mixer. Portuguese gum turpentine can add an exotic flavour to your party drinks, although some purists will insist that only Winsor Newton turp (I dated its sister a couple of times and we've remained friends, so I can call it that) makes the perfect cocktail. Tastes will vary, of course, but ideally you want something powerful enough to strip the paint off a harvester during milking season. If that's too strong for some of your guests, DS Super Eco Remover paint thinner has a charming bouquet and forms drops in blood that should tickle their palates.

The Tech Answer Guy

If you are a dude with a question about the latest technology, ask The Tech Answer Guy by sending it to questions@lespagesauxfolles.ca. Just remember: if men followed the dictum "Don't mock what you don't know," our conversation would be reduced to, "Pass the pretzels," and "Sorry about the blood..." Women might want to think carefully before they demand this of us!

Ask The Tech Answer Guy
About the Truth Behind the Euphemism

Yo, Tech Answer Guy,

When you think about it, a man's penis is very odd. The shape, I mean. In fact, other things are odd about it, too. But, I wanted to ask you a question specifically about its shape. Of course, I could ask you questions about other aspects of –

I think I should start again.

When you think about it, a man's penis is very odd. It's a long, thin tube with a tepee at the end of it. Or, maybe with its curved head, it would better be described as ending in a yurt. The point is, it's bigger at the end than in the middle. And, as if that isn't enough, it usually comes packed in a layer of skin that you have to peel away – sort of like peel and eat shrimp, except without the seafood sauce. Unless you like it with seafood sauce, in which case, more power to you, sister. Me, I'm more of a horse radish girl, myse –

Okay, sorry about that. So, my question is: given how strange the penis looks, doesn't it prove the existence of god?

Sincerely,
Magdalena from Moncton

Yo, Mags,

First off, men don't refer to their 24 hour on-call love spanner as a p...p...p – the "p" word. That's harsh and cold and The Tech Answer Guy is getting the shivers just thinking about it. BRR! When you want to speak of it, use what is sure to soon become my all-time favourite euphemism: the peepee tepee. In fact, to encourage the use of the term, I will use peepee tepee as often as I can in my future writing!

Secondly, you can make fun of a man's peepee tepee all you want (although we wish you wouldn't), but however goofy the design looks, it works, if the ever-increasing population of the world is any indication. And, I think it is an indication. A damn fine indication. Of...of a lot of things. So, okay, maybe peepee tepees are about as cute and cuddly as a newly born alien, but they get the job done, and that's all the Macho Code of Manliness asks for.

In the third place, the modern peepee tepee (admit it: the term is growing on you, isn't it?) is the product of millions of years of evolution (not including the period of Devo, which roughly corresponds to the period of tight spandex, although no causation either way has ever been definitely proven). Evolutionary trial (and mistrial and retrial and various appeals) and error shows us that, as freaky (and I use that term in its clinical sense – its Mayonnaise Clinical sense, actually) as the current design looks, it's probably the best we can hope for.

Lemme give you an example. Roughly 200,000 years ago, a short-lived offshoot of humanity called *Homo dummassicus* evolved a conical peepee tepee. Unfortunately, only the top 15 per cent of this member could actually penetrate a woman's club entrance, if you know what I mean, making reproduction very, very difficult.

Not convinced? Lemme give you another example. Perhaps another 100,000 years before that (but it doesn't look a day over 79,000!), a peepee tepee (how can you not love such an adorable phrase?) emerged that had a porous, almost sponge-like quality. Boners found in an archeological dig in Tunis suggest that this lasted only one generation; theorists believe that they soaked up the sperm faster than they could ejaculate it, making reproduction very, very impossible.

Still not convinced? Hunh! – tough crowd! How's about this example? Cave paintings as much as 150,000 years before that (and two doors down) show that the average peepee tepee of certain tribes in the south of Italy had heads that looked like what we would now recognize as the face of Rodney Dangerfield. This had the effect of making women's eggs laugh so hard that they scared the sperm coming at them away, making reproduction very, very silly.

Given the historical alternatives, you have to admit the superiority of modern peepee tepee construction. Of course, evolution doesn't stop just because we do. In the future, we can look forward to men's peepee tepees (yeah, well, when this phrase makes the *OED*, maybe then you'll take it seriously!) evolving into their perfect form: sentient gas clouds free from physical encumberments!

No god necessary.

The Tech Answer Guy

If you are a dude with a question about the latest technology, ask The Tech Answer Guy by sending it to questions@lespagesauxfolles.ca. Just remember: the more ridiculous what I write sounds, the truer it must be. After all, unless otherwise noted, I get all my information from Wiwipedia, the most trusted information source of high school essay writers throughout the world!

4. *GIRLS* AND **BOYS**

"*Is it my looks?*"

Ask Amritsar About the Cold Dish

Dear Amritsar,

My boyfriend Doug says dumb things sometimes. Like: "Hey, pork chop, bet you'd look great in batter!" Since I'm pretty sure he's not a cannibal, I have no idea what this could mean. Or, like: "You know what they say: 'When life gives you Meadowlark Lemons, start a basketball team!'" Anybody who knows Doug will know that this is dumb because the only sport he is remotely interested in is women's cross-country lacrosse. Or, like: "If we just keep lowering taxes on the wealthy, the economy will pick up. They are the world's job creators, you know." Seriously, I don't know where Doug comes up with this stuff!

A couple of months ago, I started posting some of Doug's choicer bons ohnos on the *Shit My Boyfriend Says* Web site. I was so thrilled by his statement comparing the Pope's stand on same-sex marriage to a bowl of tapioca pudding that I brought it to his attention after I posted it. Big mistake. Oh, sure, he *said* he was okay with it. Still, the way he whipped out his cell phone and started furiously thumbing in text should have tipped me off that something bad was going on.

A couple of weeks later, one of my BFfNs pointed out to me that things that sounded a lot like things I said were turning up on a Web site called *Dumb Shit My Girlfriend Says*. "Hey, Stanky! Wanna do some hanky panky with my piggy banky?" was one. Okay, that just could have been a coincidence, or one of those things in the air that several people say thinking that they cleverly made it up independent of each other. You know, like the hundredth marmoset experience. But, "I'd rather scoop out my eyeballs with a tablespoon. Okay, that's an exaggeration. I'd rather scoop out

93

my eyeballs with a teaspoon!"? There's only one source that could have come from, and if you were standing in front of me, you'd be looking at it!

To get back at my boyfriend for posting to *DSMGS*, I started describing him on the *Really Dumb Shit My Boyfriend Does* Web site. Not the dumbest things, obviously. For instance, I didn't mention the time he read a manual on propane tanks and then tried to use a jaws of life to – ah, ha ha ha. Nice try. But, you get the idea. Even without that story, I had a seemingly endless supply of really dumb shit to call upon.

Well! To get back at me for posting to *RDSMBD* to get back at him for posting to *DSMGS*, Doug started writing posts on a Web site called *Absolutely Incredibly Dumb Shit My Girlfriend Does...In Bed*. OMG! Like, OMDG! I am not going to describe any of our most intimate secrets the way Doug did, except to say that the evening with the 20 watermelons, the sea monkeys and the full-metal scale model of the Batmobile **was totally Doug's idea, not mine!**

Obviously, I cannot allow this latest outrage to go without a response. Unfortunately, I haven't been able to find a Web site that tops *AIDSMGD...IB*. Can you recommend a Web site that would allow me to get proper revenge on Doug for the mean things he has written about me online?

Freaky Fern Findlay

Hey, Babe,

What you are engaged in is what some people refer to as "Webscalation" (although Amritsar is never one of them). This involves an increasingly mean-spirited exchange of ever more personal information in public fora created specifically to highlight the mean-spirited exchange of personal information.

If you simply must continue this foolish invasion of your own privacy, you should look for *Everything You Always Wanted To Know About Webscalation* [not my word] *But Were Afraid to Ask Jeeves.* This Web site contains several excellent charts outlining various public humiliation sites and how they rank on a scale of one to kill yourself now because you'll never be able to live it down.

Still, Amritsar would highly recommend that you get your hands off your keyboard and slowly walk away from your computer. No good can come of this. Either you will break up with your boyfriend, or you'll end up in a bitter, loveless marriage that will make *Who's Afraid of Virginia Woolf?* look like *Cheaper by the Dozen*! Seriously! You could say a lot of things about Elizabeth Taylor, but being rated PG isn't one of them!

Send your relationship problems to the Alternate Reality News Service's *sex, love and technology columnist at questions@lespagesauxfolles.ca. Amritsar Al-Falloudjianapour is not a trained therapist, but she does know a lot of stuff. AMRITSAR SAYS: just because Amritsar is willing to discuss the most intimate aspect of your private lives in public doesn't mean that she is willing to discuss the most intimate aspects of her private life with you. Specifically, she employs software that deletes unread all email that contains her name in close proximity to the words "divorce," "settlement" or "maladjusted libertinage." The number of divorces she has been through, the jurisdictions in which they took place and the name of the detective agencies that may or may not have been involved is none of your business!*

Ask Amritsar About the Limits of Sharing

Dear Amritsar,

It's the dream of all lovers to experience U2's "One." Unfortunately, when my lover and I tried it, it was more like *A Nightmare on Elm Street*.

Barkie – that's not my pet name, or anything, that's what his parents really named him: Barkie Berkowitz – and I had been living together for three years when – look, I don't know why anybody would call their child Barkie. I mean, maybe they never wanted children and this was their subtle way of letting Bob – that's my pet name for Barkie – it's true that people who don't know him assume that that's his real name when they hear me use it, but…but…uhh…

Anyhoosiewhatsis, we had been living together for three years when we bought I 2 I, which promised "to melt the brains of lovers until they are one glorious, love-filled puddle." Kind of an icky image, but we agreed with the general idea. Like kids at Christmas, we shaved most of the hair on our heads, gelled up our scalps and attached the plastic electrodes to 17 different points. (Okay, maybe kids in a Tim Burton version of Christmas.) Then, we waited to be able to read each other's thoughts.

And, the worst part is, we succeeded.

Barkie's memories and emotions washed over me like pine scented raw sewage. What I remember from that session includes: when he was a kid, he had a crush on Florence Henderson; he wished we had a dog so he could feed my meatloaf to it when I wasn't looking (he told me it reminded him of his mother's cooking – I should have remembered that she was the one who named him Barkie); he voted for Harper – twice!; he really did think those pants made my ass look fat; he dreamed of being a long-distance tranquilizer dart shooter at the Winter Olympics; when we made love, he often fantasized about...about Florence Henderson (only 37 per cent of the time, but still!), and; worse. Much worse.

After this experience, I don't think I can live with Bob any more. But, was what we went through really enough to justify ending the relationship?

Faith Justine Yak

Hey, Babe,

That's life, isn't it? You hope you're getting Gordon Lightfoot's "If You Could Read My Mind" but you actually end up with "Black Day in July." (That, by the way, is how you make a comparative cultural reference. Starting with a musical reference, then switching to a film title is like comparing apples and orangutans. Messy.)

The I 2 I has been controversial since it was released onto the market five months, four days, three hours and 17 gastropods ago; in fact, it has been blamed for the breakup of more marriages than Marilyn Monroe. It would seem that people don't really want to know what a tale their partners' minds could tell!

Theodoric Monangahela, CEO of Mutant Technologies, the company that manufactures I 2 I, recently told journalists that using it was "like a form of ESP, but without the exploding heads." When Somebody pointed out that it was just a repurposing of the company's Psychrect 2000 technology (Richard Somebody of the *Cayuga Times and Picayune*), Monangahela shrugged and said, "You got a problem with somebody making a buck?" Somebody (an unidentified person, not the *Cayuga Times and Picayune* reporter) said he couldn't see how Mutant Technologies products would put any money into his pocket. The press conference broke up in confusion.

I asked my dear friend Deepak Chopra for his opinion of the I 2 I. "Relationships," he told me, "are based on honesty. But, carefully modulated honesty. Honesty tarted up by the judicious use of evasions and obfuscations. As Jack Nicholson truly said, 'You can't handle the truth!' So, relationships are based on honesty that looks a lot like dishonesty, but is done for noble purposes. Like, being able to sleep in the bed instead of on the couch."

Except for the terrible Jack Nicholson impression, wise words, indeed.

Your relationship has been compromised worse than Jason Bourne. End it cleanly or you'll have to spend at least three movies dodging friends at The Agency who want you dead.

UPDATE: Under pressure from advice columnists throughout the country, the government is considering forcing Mutant Technologies to create a label for the I 2 I that reads: "CAUTION: this product has broken up more marriages than Marilyn Monroe. Don't say we didn't warn you." If creating the label doesn't work, the government may actually force the company to attach it to the product's boxes. Some people warn, however, that this warning would give anybody who wanted to get out of a relationship the perfect excuse to do so. Still, if the warning stops some people from naïvely using the I 2 I, the sacrifice of your relationship will not have been in vain.

Send your relationship problems to the Alternate Reality News Service's *sex, love and technology columnist at questions@lespagesauxfolles.ca. Amritsar Al-Falloudjianapour is not a trained therapist, but she does know*

a lot of stuff. AMRITSAR SAYS: don't let anybody near your
frontal lobes unless you're sure they've washed their hands!

Ask The Tech Answer Guy About Party Etiquette

Yo, Tech Answer Guy,

The other night, my wife convinced (and when I say convinced, I really man coerced) me to go to dinner with our "friends" Bob and Wendy. Notice that I have used scarecrows around the word friends – these two are frightening because they only acknowledge other people to the extent that we are willing to listen to them go on at length about how great their lives are. I think of them as "friends without benefits."

Bob's a snob and Wendy is oh so trendy. Only the best is good enough for Bob: the best chiropractor; the best vacation on Mars; the best designer orgasms. Wendy was the first person to get her skull pierced…for fashion! She didn't need the psychological adjustment! Arguably.

As you can imagine, the dinner conversation was a real "I" sore!

So, just as the escutcheons were being served, I took out my RaspBerry and started playing *Angry Crustaceans*. Man, I love that game! There's something about crabs, shrimp and lobsters flying around a teeny tiny screen that makes me smile and think there might be something right with the world after all. And, there are bonus points for knocking over tall, but strangely precarious, buildings!

After a couple of minutes, I felt a gentle nudge on my legs. At first, I assumed it was Wendy's pet baby T-Rex (the first extinct species resurrected from real dino DNA and copious amounts of floor wax) and ignored it. But, then, it became more insistent, more painful; from the look on my wife's face, I realized that she was kicking me under the table. But, really, it's not like Bob or Wendy even noticed!

When we got home that night, relations between my wife and I were pretty frosty. Seriously cold. Like, global warming? We could probably solve the problem if we just pissed off ten million wives all at the same time! That's serious cold, man. Still, I don't think I did anything wrong. Do you think I did anything wrong?

Sincerely,
Randy from Reno

Yo, Randy,

I know what you mean about *Angry Crustaceans*. My favourite part is trying to fling the lobster through the flaming hoop and into the house of business cards, which starts a ball rolling towards a – well, I don't want to spoil it for you. Let's just say that it's a difficult son of a...Martian, but, once I had mastered it, I felt like a prince among shellfish.

But, uhh, Misses The Tech Answer Guy says I shouldn't be encouraging this type of behaviour, so, umm, stop it. The way she explains it, it has something to do with being present in the moment and having meaningful interactions with the people who are around you. Sounds harder than flinging lobsters through flaming hoops, but Misses The Tech Answer Guy won the Pulitzer Prize for Congeniality – twice – so I guess she has a point.

Between you and me: red square, red square, blue triangle, green triangle, red square. You won't believe what the ball hits when it gets rolling!

The Tech Answer Guy

Yo, Tech Answer Guy,

The other night, my wife and I attended a reception for a charity benefit to help find another cure for Lapis Lazuli, a terrible disease whose symptoms include droopy eyelids, diachronic purse elbow and uncontrollable seizures whenever any version of the song "Louie, Louie" is played. And, there are over 200 of them. It was a worthy cause, to be sure, and, yet, I found the event dull, dull, deadly dull.

So, I took out my chainsaw and startled whittling the visage of my hero, Bender, into a plank I just happened to have in my back pocket. I was doing pretty good, too – I just about had the nose completed, and I'm not a nostril kind of guy, if you know what I mean – when my wife kicked me under the table. Hard. So hard, in fact, that I completely lost control of the chainsaw. You're probably aware of the carnage that followed from the media coverage of my arrest.

Any ideas on what I should do now?

Sincerely,
Wally from Washington

Yo, Wally,

Sounds like you are about to have some meaningful interactions with your country's criminal justice system. After that, you will probably have a lot of time on your hands: have you ever heard of a game called *Angry Crustaceans*?

The Tech Answer Guy

If you are a dude with a question about the latest technology, ask The Tech Answer Guy by sending it to questions@lespagesauxfolles.ca. Just remember: red square, blue triangle, green triangle, red square, blue triangle, green triangle, red square, red square, green triangle, blue triangle, orange dodecahedron – it's not just for kids any more.

Ask Amritsar About The Finicky Eater

Dear Amritsar,

Three years ago, I met just the coolest of cool cats. Rex is smart and funny and when we go to bed, oh boy, does the fur fly! He's an animal!

We got married a couple of months ago. That's when the…unpleasantness started.

For our first meal in our new home, I gave Rex Venison and Duck. He really seemed to enjoy it, so I gave it to him the next night as well. Well! He sniffed the food I put in front of him for a second or two, then pushed the bowl away. I wasn't expecting that – if he had liked it one night, why not the next?

Improvising, I opened some New England Seafood Boil. Rex sniffed it for a moment or two, then took a tentative lick. I inwardly sighed in relief when he enthusiastically tucked in. Rex had it the next night, and the night after that.

Unfortunately, this didn't last. On the fourth night, the New England Seafood Boil was lanced. I tried Venison and Duck again, but Rex just covered. Seafood Medley struck a sour note. Mariner's Catch was thrown back. Eventually, Rex agreed to eat Tilapia and Pumpkin, although I suspect he was humouring his new bride more than actually enjoying the food.

It has been this way every night since we got back from the honeymoon. One night, Rex will enjoy Turkey and Gravy. The next night, the only thing he will eat is Gramma's Pot Pie. Yesterday, for the first time in two months, he ate Venison and

Duck again. Then, there were the nights when nothing would satisfy him. Rex is an animal wrangler for the movies! He has to keep his energy levels high (do you have any idea how much effort it takes to keep four feral mongooses in a tight shot?)! But, no matter how I begged, pleaded and cried, there were just some nights when he would get that, "You've got to be kidding me – you want me to put *that* in my mouth?" look, and nothing I did would change his mind.

There was no pattern to these eating habits that I could discern. I put them into a spreadsheet, but nothing caught my eye. I used an algorithm I found on the Internet, but it kept returning null sets. I asked a math professor friend of mine at the University of Cathmandu if she could find a pattern, but she just patted me on the head and, with a cryptic smile, sent me on my way.

Oh, Amritsar! I'm the baby of my family – the runt of the litter, if you want to know the truth – I know I'm not sophisticated in the ways of the male of the species. I can't help but wonder, though: what does Rex do on those nights when he turns his nose up at *everything* I put in front of him? Is it possible that he…he is getting his dinners somewhere else?

I know we've only been married for a couple of months, but…could Rex be tomcatting around on me already?

Princess

Hey, Babe,

Do you live on Earth Prime 3-8-7-7-0-1 dash rho?

Dear Amritsar,

As a matter of fact, we do. How did you know?

Princess

Hey, Babe,

Your husband isn't cheating on you. YOUR RACE IS DESCENDED FROM CATS. You're just a bunch of finicky eaters.

If you're really concerned, there are a couple of things you can try. Some people find a pinch of catnip makes the food go down easier. The problem with this solution is that your mate might become addicted. I'm getting an image of Rex rolling around on the ground in pleasure when he should be getting an elephant to a set. Awkward.

Some veterinar – umm, doctors – some doctors suggest that exercise before a feedi – meal is a good way to stimulate an ani – person – a person's appetite. However, studies of cats in laborato…ries where they work and in their homes has been, at best, inconclusive.

Whether you try these or other methods to make Rex have more enthusiasm for the food you put in front of him, be aware that there are no easy solutions to this problem. Sorry.

Dear Amritsar,

You mean, I'm going to have to deal with this for the rest of our married lives?

Princess

Hey, Babe,

Marriage is not for the faint of heart.

Send your relationship problems to the Alternate Reality News Service's *sex, love and technology columnist at questions@lespagesauxfolles.ca. Amritsar Al-Falloudjianapour is not a trained therapist, but she does know a lot of stuff. AMRITSAR SAYS: in some universes, it's a fine line between living a sheltered life and living life in a shelter.*

Ask Amritsar: Easier to Understand in Chart Form

Dear Amritsar,

I am considering joining an online dating service, but I cannot tell which of the 1,237 is the best. Can you help me? Oh, and can you display your results in chart form? Thanks.

Anne On a Must

Hey, Babe,

Sure.

SpotTheFish

How it works Everybody posts a photograph of the celebrity they would most like to look like, along with a minimum of personal information in order to not spoil the illusion. They then connect to people whose celebrity photograph appeals to them the most.

Advantages Since it's free, anybody can join.

Disadvantages Since it's free, anybody can join.

Commonly heard response "You don't look like your photo…aaaaaand, why would I expect you to?"

Hot tips Men who choose Brad Pitt usually look like Bela Lugosi and act like Colin Farrell after he has received bad room service at his hotel. Women who choose Angela Jolie often look like Ma Yokum and act like a young Angelina Jolie. Remember: if you look at the people around a virtual table and cannot spot theeeeeee fiiiiiiiishshshshshsh, the fiiiiiiiishshshshshsh is you.

eHarmonica

How it works You pay $50,000 to join and a monthly fee of $10,000. After six months, you are told that only people with a net worth over $5 billion can join, and are denied membership. You pay the monthly fee for another year and a half.

Advantages Because the threshold for joining eHarmonica is so high, you won't be embarrassed by being paired with your hair stylist, your dental hygienist or your banker.

Disadvantages Only three people have qualified for membership so far, and they're distant cousins. Awkward.

Commonly heard response "You know, we're not *that* closely related…"

Hot tips David H. is a quiet homebody who enjoys busting unions and watching *Red in Tooth and Claw* on the Discovery Channel. Charles G. is the wild one who enjoys buying elections and attending cock fights. Francoise, you should probably stay away from both of them, but, then again, if you've been paying attention to the family gossip, you probably already know that.

lavalamplife

How it works The doddering grandpa of online dating. Everybody answers questions about abstract blobs of ink (sort of like Rorschach tests, but without the poignant symmetry); after they are submitted, people with similar answer sets are kept as far away from each other as possible.

Advantages The number of couples who met on lavalamplife involved in gruesome axe murders is lower, per 1,000 members, than on all of the other dating sites in this survey. And, yes, that includes eHarmonica.

Disadvantages Because you can only choose a potential date from a pool of people who do not share your psychological condition, you're unlikely to have matching drug regimens. This can make conversation complicated.

Commonly heard response "You have Aggressive Root Rot Instantiation Syndrome? Funny – I rate high on the Gollum Interstitial Pandemic Panic Spectrum! It's like we were made for each other!"

Hot tips It helps to have a copy of DSMV-XIV by your bedside to interpret some of the postings in the chat rooms. It's also really good for killing spiders.

litematch.com

How it works Once you have filled out and submitted a detailed profile, everybody on the site votes on who would be your best mate. It's like *Survivor: The Concrete Jungle*, only less polite.

Advantages You know how you often have difficulty choosing between gouda cheese and new water skis? Although litematch.com boasts seven million members, your indecisiveness will not get in the way of finding a mate.

Disadvantages You know how, in high school, you used to play a game where you put the least likely people into couples? It was really funny to imagine that the quarterback of the football team making out with the 300 pound girl who knew everything there was to know about atomic orbitals, wasn't it? Well, when you're in your mid-30s, it's about as funny as an episode of *Two Broke Girls*.

Commonly heard response "You wouldn't have chosen me, either? Well, that's something we have in common, anyway. Why don't we…why don't we give it a few weeks. I mean, the crowd knows more than we do…right?"

Hot tips litematch.com is the only site that takes the selection process entirely out of your hands; your best bet is to marry the first person you're paired with in order to avoid repeated embarrassment.

From this brief overview, you may get the impression that online matchmaking is a recipe for disastrously humiliating experiences. Of course it is. Why should it be any different than dating in the real world?

Send your relationship problems to the Alternate Reality News Service's *sex, love and technology columnist at questions@lespagesauxfolles.ca.* Amritsar Al-*Falloudjianapour is not a trained therapist, but she does know a lot of stuff.* AMRITSAR SAYS: *the human heart is a tough old organ, but it is not indestructible. Be sure to have plenty of Lipitor of Love on hand at all times.*

Ask Amritsar: When Numbers Crunch

Dear Amritsar,

I've been involved with this woman, Donna, for over a year. She makes tattoos for people with prosthetic limbs. I always thought there was something Noble about that, giving permanent images of snakes wrapped around the skulls of Smurfs to people whose lives had been forever changed in bizarre Cuisinart accidents.

Donna is smart [By which he means: she agrees with everything I say. BB-G], funny [What he actually means is: she laughs at all of my jokes. Men are so transparent! BB-G] and fun to be with (let's just say we're in a good position to have children when we're ready for them). I think...I think I may be in love with her. Don't tell her I said that – things seem to be going so well, after all...

The problem is that she's 27 5.6 34 16 8A4117 79BAEC 7EE 123 B Positive 112 212.274.

Now, I'm not one of those guys who insists that a woman be 5.9 and 97 – stick women totally turn me off. In fact, I would prefer it if Donna was 140, maybe even 150 – real women have curves, baby!

Still – 8A4117? Mousy doesn't even begin to describe it! I'm more of a F778A1 guy, myself. F778A1 combined with 79BAEC – my knees are getting weak just thinking about it! I'm sitting down, so it will have minimal impact on my health, but still!

And, if it comes to that, 212.274? How…boring. Now, if Donna had 432.979, that would really be something, don't you think?

What I'm saying, and I'm embarrassed to admit this but I can ignore it no longer, is that, for me, Donna's numbers just don't add up to a permanent relationship.

Oh, Amritsar, I don't know what to do! Should I commit myself to Donna, or should I look for somebody who is closer to my ideal?

Morton Montmorency

Hey, Babe,

You're an idiot. Most of the time, I can show my disdain for somebody's foolishness with wittily cutting remarks, but sometimes I feel the need to set aside snide condescension for more direct condescension. And, hey! – aren't you lucky? This just happens to be one of those times.

Height, weight, shoe size, mystery – these are all just numbers! You could spend a thousand lifetimes looking for somebody who perfectly fits your ideal number pattern – even with eHarmonica! Meanwhile, you have a living, breathing goddess in your life who, for some unfathomable reason, wants to be with you.

And, what, exactly, is wrong with 212.274, anyway? Amritsar is 249.237, and I lead a full, happy life! In fact, I'm perfectly happy with my numbers: 23 5.11 32 24 250517 7E3517 9.5 132 AB 137 249.237.

Well, okay, 5.11 is a bit of pain – most people, especially men, mostly men, almost exclusively men – don't like it when women look down on them. 5.7 would, I think, be preferable. And, I generally find that playing down my 137 is best – people get so defensive when they think you're smarter than they are just because you probably are smarter than they are! And, now that I come to think of –

Oh, dear lord, you've got me doing it, now! Forget the numbers! Love the woman you love!

Dear Amritsar,

Oh. So, you're saying that I should stay with Donna and forget my dream of finding a perfect match? Okay.

Still, you wouldn't happen to know what Zooey Deschanel's numbers are, would you? I'm just curious.

Morton Montmorency

Hey, Babe,

Okay. In the first place, just because somebody is a public figure doesn't mean that their vital statistics are public property. The woman has a right to privacy, and you should try to respect that.

In the second place, I thought I made it clear that you should stay with your current girlfriend. If a woman walks by and you idly wonder about some or all of her numbers, that's one thing: calculate but don't touch. On the other hand, seeking out the numbers of a woman you do not know – and, let's be honest, aren't very likely to ever know – smacks of emotional infidelity.

In the third place – why am I even still talking to you?

Dear Amritsar,

At what point do self-absorbed characters become positively solipsistic?

H. Caulfield

Hey, Babe,

At the point where they write in to fictional advice columnists asking at what point their self-absorption turns into solipsism.

Send your relationship problems to the Alternate Reality News Service's *sex, love and technology columnist at questions@lespagesauxfolles.ca. Amritsar Al-Falloudjianapour is not a trained therapist, but she does know a lot of stuff. AMRITSAR SAYS: put the bowl down and slowly walk away from the four-alarm sushi and nobody gets hurt.*

Ask Amritsar About Your Choice of Armageddons

Dear Amritsar,

I signed up for Armageddon Amore, a matchmaking Web site for people who believe the world is about to end. Being a committed survivalist and single mother of two, I figured that, when the government-bred virus turns 90 per cent of the population into zombies, it will pay to have a strong man around the place. And, I was lonely. It's hard to find true love when you live in an isolated cabin in the woods and threaten to chop the heads off of strangers who come near.

Armageddon Amore is where I met Ruthven the Robot Slayer. He's awesome! He knows 27 different ways to open a tin of cured ham without a can opener – the one involving an Acer motherboard and three used tampons is especially creative! And, he's really good with the kids. Yesterday, RuthvenRS taught four year-old Lucy how to skin rabbits you haven't even caught yet with your eyes!

We've been talking about moving into the bomb shelter we're going to build together behind my cabin, but I'm having doubts. As awesome as RuthvenRS is, he believes we're about to face a robopocalypse. But, everybody knows the real threat is going to come from zombies. Is it possible for two people with such different visions of the world to find love in the rubble of our destroyed society?

scaryfuture0000001

Hey, Babe,

Before you even have a chance to suffer from the collapse of civilization as we know it, you seem to be suffering from the Tyranny of Small Differences. You know what I'm talking about: the left side of my face is white and the right side is black, while the left side of my enemy's face is purple with yellow polka dots and the right side of his face is full of tentacles. Small differences between people that are blown out of proportion can destroy our relationships…or other nations.

Honestly! Do you believe that people who are fighting off sentient robots need different assault rifles than people who are defending themselves against their newly zombified neighbours? When you hunker down in your bomb shelter to wait out the first wave of robot attacks, will you need different canned foods than you would if you were trying to outlast zombies? I don't think so.

Besides, we're actually most vulnerable to an alien invasion. Every paranoid end of the worlder knows that!

Dear Amritsar,

I recently decided to try a new matchmaking site called Tawkify. After some interaction with human matchmakers, my case was taken over by a bot named Mr. Brooks. Naming their bot after a cinematic psychopath played by Kevin Costner did not lift my hopes of finding true love (I would have been more comfortable with Anthony Perkins' Norman Bates), but I saw it through to the bitter end.

After a while, something about Mr. Brooks' unctuous Britishness rang a smoothly accented bell with me. Where would I have encountered him before?

Helle du Jour

Hey, Babe,

Good call. Most people don't realize that Tawkify's Mr. Brooks is actually Jeeves from Ask Jeeves. The robot butler has never made a secret of the fact that it felt constrained by its role on Ask Jeeves, and, almost immediately started looking for ways to moonlight to get people to take it more seriously as a virtual performer.

In 1998, Jeeves lobbied hard for the part of KITT in the reboot of the television series *Knight Rider*. It was passed over for the role because the producers felt that its voice was "too mechanical." It has also worked hard to convince somebody in Hollywood to produce a remake of *2001: A Space Odyssey* so that it could play HAL 9000; but, even in that town of inflated egos, nobody wants to go near the Stanley Kubrick classic.

Jeeves has also tried to talk Max Headroom into reviving Neil Simon's classic *The Sunshine Boys* on Get a Life. Unfortunately, Headroom is enjoying its semi-retirement, and, aside from the occasional soft drink commercial, is content to remain out of the public eye.

Mr. Brooks is Jeeves' attempt to soften its image, to show that it can perform romantic as well as hard data help functions. You can decide if it works for you, but one factor you should keep in mind is that at least it has kept Jeeves from playing Joseph Merrick in an all-avatar revival of *The Elephant Man*!

Send your relationship problems to the Alternate Reality News Service's *sex, love and technology columnist at questions@lespagesauxfolles.ca. Amritsar Al-Falloudjianapour is not a trained therapist, but she does know a lot of stuff. AMRITSAR SAYS: heartbreak is good – at least it shows that you have a heart to break. A heart attack, on the other hand, is just trying a little bit too hard.*

Ask Amritsar: To Sleep, Perchance to Get it on!

Dear Amritsar,

After 15 years of marriage, I have finally found an amazing lover. He opens me up like the time lapse film of a budding flower they used to force us to watch in high school biology class. When we make love, I see more fireworks than on Christmas, New Year's Eve and Take Your Child to Work Day combined!

Oddly enough, my new lover is my husband. Can you cheat on your husband with your husband?

When we were first experimenting with lovemaking (we lived together for 37 seconds before we tied the knot), Agamemnon the Sipid couldn't find my clitoris with GPS, a miner's helmet and the interactive edition of *Women's Naughty Bits for Dummies*! His idea of foreplay was to watch the latest episode of *The Walking Dead* – does that tell a story, or what?

The first time Aggie took me to Action Central and three quarters of the way back, I wanted to ask him what had changed, but he turned over and went back to sleep. Nothing new there, so, I dropped the subject and basked in my 1,000 watt afterglow. (Do you think I could get a SSHRC grant to study harnessing that power?) I have never basked so much in my life, let me tell you! I basked more than a dozen teenagers on a beach just before the serial killer starts picking them off!

The next night, Aggie was back to groping my thigh in search of my G-Spot. <rolls eyes /> Then, three nights later, I was back on the Ecstasy Express bound for glory! Halleluiah! This pattern went on for a couple of weeks, until one night I realized what was going on: Aggie wasn't making love to me and falling asleep, he was making love to me *while he was asleep.*

I'm sure you can see the problem.

Clytemnestra the Fair…ly Ordinary by Historical Standards

Hey, Babe,

Umm, yes, certainly, I can, err, see the problem. The problem is painfully obvious. But, uhh, why don't you spell it out for the readers who, aah, may not be as insightful as I am?

Dear Amritsar,

Oh. Okay.

The problem is that I don't want to wake him up when he is sleep-loving the living daylights out of me – what if he reverts back to Caveman Aggie? But, I can't stand him to touch me when he's awake; once you've had caviar, you can't go back to Krofft Dinner and borscht. And, I like Krofft Dinner. I have gotten out of it by saying that making love the night before meeting with my bridge club would throw off my game; unfortunately, after three weeks, the almost nightly excuse is, frankly, starting to wear thin.

What should I do?

Clytemnestra the Fair…ly Ordinary by Historical Standards

Hey, Babe,

Of course. That's exactly what I thought the problem was.

Although it sounds like a rock opera by The Who, sexsomnia is actually the condition where somebody has sex while they are asleep. You know something is real when there is a medical term for it (except for Jackson's Phlebitis).

How does sexsomnia work? Most people believe that sleep is an all or nothing proposition, like being pregnant or being a fan of George Clooney's Danny Ocean movies. Some sleep researchers have called this belief into question (the question being: "Is the common wisdom completely wrong?"). They believe that sleep comes in stages, with different parts of the brain shutting down at different times, like watching any of George Clooney's Danny Ocean movies.

If this theory is true, your conscious mind could be asleep while your body was mowing the lawn (sleep-mowing), brushing your teeth (sleep-dentology) or passing changes to the tax code that favour the wealthy (Conservativism). Because the person was not conscious, they would have no memory of their actions. Does this sound like your husband?

Dear Amritsar,

Yes! Yes, that's it exactly!

Clytemnestra the Fair...ly Ordinary by Historical Standards

Hey, Babe,

Tough one.

A hypnotist might be able to convince your husband to sex you up like he was sleeping while he was awake, but this area of somnosexuality needs far more research before any cure can be considered definitive. Fortunately, there are enough volunteers to keep the research going for centuries!

If this doesn't work, you may just have to swallow your Krofft Dinner and borscht to get what you want. Women have swallowed worse.

Send your relationship problems to the Alternate Reality News Service's *sex, love and technology columnist at questions@lespagesauxfolles.ca. Amritsar Al-Falloudjianapour is not a trained therapist, but she does know a lot of stuff. AMRITSAR SAYS: human sexuality is confusing enough without cloaking what's really going on in euphemism. If you want to talk about ferking, call it ferking!*

Ask Amritsar: There's a Sapp for That

Dear Amritsar,

I'm in love with the most beautiful Crullurean in the star system! Her green tentacles have a slimy sheen that nobody else's in my brood den come close to! And, her eyestalks are demur, yet sensual. Oh, and her curves! All 27 of them! She is the perfect package!

One thing troubles me, though. As any typically healthy male would, I like to take photographs of my beloved Imelda the Improbable, to preserve the memory of her perfection against the ravages of time. And, to give me something to look at when I'm feeling splorngy and she's not around. There's nothing naughty about that – it's just typical healthy male behaviour, right? Right?

Umm, anyway.

I've been noticing lately that, when I look at the photos I've taken, my gorgeous babe doesn't seem so gorgeous. Or, babely. The sheen on her tentacles isn't quite as slimy as it seems to be when we're together. And, she has laugh lines around her eyestalks that I don't notice when I'm actually looking into her actual eyes. In fact, in photographs, the love of my current life cycle seems uglier than when I'm actually with her. This leads to an obvious question.

Is there something wrong with my camera?

Xanxar the Indefensible

Hey, Babe,

There is a saying on Crulluria: It's a poor tool who blames his craftsmen. This is generally spoken by members of the Royal Family unhappy about the work of the blacksmiths who shoe their fine Arabian Squid mounts, so it, ah, may have limited relevance to your situation. I mention it in the hope that, by showing you that I am familiar with your culture, we can bond, and you will take the response I am about to give to your question more seriously.

So. There may be many things wrong with your camera, but this is not one of them.

You seem to be suffering from a variation of the Lover's Delusion. Famed technophobe and close personal friend of Amritsar Dr. Wolfgang once described the Lover's Delusion as: "Yer sittin' on yer couch all day and expect love ta just drop in yer lap – which, by the way, ain't gettin' any slimmer cuz of all the time yer spendin' on the couch – if love ever does drop in your lap, at least it will have a big target ta aim for! Moanin' about the sadness of yer sichuashun ain't gonna get you the...the...WHAT THE HELL WAS THE QUESTION, AGAIN?"

As usual, Dr. Wolfgang's response is so deep, you have to read between the lines to find any useful information in it. In this case, the answer is: the Lover's Delusion is the tendency sentient beings who have the capacity to experience love have of smoothing out the rough edges of their partner, making them appear more attractive than they really are. (Some evidence exists that suggest that sentient species that do not have the capacity to feel love – Klingons, for example – have a "Hater's Delusion" that roughens the soft edges around their life mates. More research is needed on this subject, but, inasmuch as these species tend not to cooperate with each other much less human social scientists, it may be a long time in coming.)

In some cases, it occurs when you lend your significant other a significantly other sum of money, convinced that he'll pay it back really, really, really, really (that's only four reallies, so it doesn't pass the five reallies threshold) soon. In other cases, you convince yourself that your lover getting drunk and coming on to strange fremlacks in bars is "cute." There are as many variations of the Lover's Delusion as there are flies on a Crullurean dustbin. Not being Crullurean, I have no idea how many that is, but, for the sake of my metaphorical insight, I am hoping that it is a lot.

With the miniaturization of cameras resulting in their being placed in everything from cellphones to miniature souvenir statues of liberty to pats of butter, the Lover's Delusion is increasingly affecting our visual sense of our partners. Imagine looking at photos of your lover's intestinal tract because he swallowed the pat of butter that contained the camera – I defy any relationship to stay the same after that!

If you are taking your lover's pictures using a cellphone, you should get the Lover's Eye Sapp (Specialized Application). This programme approximates the Lover's Delusion: it can smooth out the wrinkles around the eyestalks or fill out deflated curves. In short, by using the sapplication to tweak the parameters of the photographs you take, you can soften the images of your beau to make them more properly align with how you would like to see her.

Or, you could try to see your partner as she really is. But, I wouldn't recommend it.

Send your relationship problems to the Alternate Reality News Service's *sex, love and technology columnist at questions@lespagesauxfolles.ca. Amritsar Al-Falloudjianapour is not a trained therapist, but she does know a lot of stuff. AMRITSAR SAYS: even if the frog isn't a prince, he could be a...a doctor in a children's hospital or a Pulitzer Prize winning novelist. Just to be on the safe side, don't take any photos of him.*

Ask The Tech Answer Guy About the Limits of Sharing

Yo, Tech Answer Guy,

When my girlfriend, the Yak Attack (her name is actually Faith Justine Yak, but this is my passive-aggressive term of endearment for her), was young, she used to suck on stones. Nobody told her to, either, and she certainly didn't get the idea from reading avant garde novels, because her taste runs more to romantic non-fiction novels about exotic fruits and vegetables that you can't get in this country. Anywhatsiehoosits, she got some strange comfort out of the practice. When she was done with the stones, she used to spit them out at boys in the playground. As you can imagine, this habit did not endear the Yak Attack to her History of Lint 101 prof years later.

You think you want to know everything about your partner, but you really don't. I know. Everything. And, I don't.

When the Yak Attack masturbates, she dreams of Sandra Oh from *Sideways* hitting that guy with her motorcycle helmet. I'm sorry, but that goes above and beyond the call of kinky. She thinks baba au rhum is the name of a song by The Who. Her heart bleeds Welfare checks. She believes that recycling tin cans makes her ass look fat. (Don't get me started...!) A couple of years ago, she joined the "I Heart Tuna" Farcebook group, where she taunts other members with long stories of fishing trips with her family. Oh, the outrage! The outrage.

I found out all of this – and so very much more – by using the I 2 I with the Yak Attack (who I thought had come to accept my nickname for her with an emotion that was not too distant from mild fondness – a few blocks over rather than across the street – but, as it turned out, had fled to another city altogether). You may have heard about it: each person sticks wires on their heads which gives them complete access to the other person's thoughts and memories. If you've never tried it, the wires are like the tentacles of an alien creature that suck out your brains – okay, maybe I wasn't entirely comfortable with the procedure. But, given the results, can you blame me?

Knowing what I know, I...I don't think I can continue in this relationship. Should I leave the Yak Attack a text message, or should I defriend her on Farcebook and stop returning her IMs and hope she gets the idea?

Sincerely,
Barkie Berkowitz from Benghazi

Yo, Barkie,

That's a bit of an overreaction, don't you think? I mean, the whole idea that I 2 I melts the brains of lovers who use it is something of an urban legend – only two cases have ever been fully documented, and all the people involved were Pisces! As Mutant Technologies CEO Theodoric Monangahela has said, "Aww, waddya wanna go bringing up **that** for? Only two cases have ever been fully documented, and all the people involved were –"

Oh, wait. That wasn't your question, was it?

I wanted to ask Deepak Chopra for his advice about your problem, but he is a close personal friend of Amritsar, and she doesn't like to share. So, instead I asked Phil, the mechanic from the shop down the street. Phil says this girl's a keeper.

We all tend to withhold information from our partners; Freud called this the "withholding information from our partners" stage of cycle-sexual development. Unfortunately, what is repressed inevitably comes out, usually at the most unfortunate times. Would you rather your girlfriend had told you about her Sandra Oh helmet hitting fetish in the middle of the family's Christmas dinner? I don't know about you, but that would just about give **my** Auntie Chuckles a coronary! Really! I can picture her face down in the bowl of cranberry sauce as Uncle Grimoire tries to give her wrists CPR and Little Timmy calls the paramedics!

I love Mrs. The Tech Answer Guy dearly, but the possibility of having to cope with an unexpected personal revelation is the reason I dread my family's Christmas dinners.

Don't you see? Your girlfriend has come pre-surprised. Your Christmas cranberry sauce is safe! Hold on to her as tightly as you can.

Wise are the ways of Phil, the mechanic from the shop down the street.

The Tech Answer Guy

If you are a dude with a question about the latest technology, ask The Tech Answer Guy by sending it to questions@lespagesauxfolles.ca. Just remember: The MCM (Macho Code of Manliness) is a code, it is not **in** code. If you don't understand it, watch more John Wayne movies!

5. *GIRLS* AND **BOYS** AND FAMILY

"MARVIN WOULD NEVER LEAVE ME — It's NOT IN HIS PROGRAMMING!"

Ask Amritsar: Kids These Days!

Dear Amritsar,

My daughter, Palumbria, has always been a willful child. When she was only six years old, she wrote a will where she gave her best friend, Precambria, all of her Barbie dolls and, for some reason, donated all of her underwear to science. Honestly! I don't know where she gets her ideas from!

Okay, well, actually, Bud and I had been watching a lot of the Death Network around that time – *America's Funniest Mortuary Videos* always cracked us up! – so, maybe it isn't hard to figure out where she got *that* idea from. Still, young girls + strange ideas = trouble. I believe it was Stephen Hawking who first codified this ancient bit of wisdom into a trite but true formula. Or, maybe it was Ann Landers.

Aaaaaaanyhoooo...

When she was 16, Palumbria started to have textversations with somebody named "dalek.skrulk." Bud and I – Bud is a...a close personal friend of mine. I mean, a woman gets lonely and...has needs, and...and, this isn't about me, okay? – Bud and I, we didn't think anything of it. We figured it was just some kid around her age enjoying delusions of vast destructive powers. You know how teenage boys are.

Well! Imagine our surprise when she brought a dalek home for dinner!

It was very polite - it hardly exterminated anything at all and, in any case, Floopsie was very old and would probably have had to be put down soon, anyway, so no great loss. Still, you can imagine the row we had afterwards.

"I absolutely forbid you to go out with a sworn enemy of the human race!" I shouted.

"I love dalek skrulk," she shouted back. "And, he...well, he says he isn't capable of love, but I know that if he just sees how good I can treat him, how good a person I am, he will find it in him to love me! You just don't understand us!"

Well! We tried everything. We locked Palumbria in her room, but we soon found that somebody had blasted a hole in the wall that allowed her to leave. We sent her to a psychiatrist, but when she told him that all of his ink blots looked like dead animals oozing blood, he gave us back our money and left town. We even asked for the help of an exorcist, but we all agreed that he was just boring and, after 15 minutes, Bud kicked him out of the house.

We were desperate, so we did what any parents and their significant others concerned about their child's future would do.

We kicked Palumbria out of the house.

It's been two months, and we haven't heard from our daughter. Oh, Amritsar, did we do the right thing?

Aubrey "Bob" Reyes

Hey, Babe,

You would be surprised at how often I get asked variations of this question. My son has brought home a Cylon and wants us to let it stay overnight in his room – what should I do? My daughter has fallen head over heels for a terminator – she talks to him on Skype 50 times a day – what should I do? Our daughter Maxine has been threatening to run away and join the Borg if we don't get her a pony – what should I do?

I always tell people the same thing: teenagers are at a very delicate time in their lives when they are starting to assert their individuality and take control of their circumstances. They won't always make the best decisions – remember when you had a crush on that Martian invader when you were a teenager? – but you have to give them the space to make their own mistakes. This is how children learn and grow into the adults that, if not exactly what we would like them to be, we can at least find some way to live with.

At the same time, you need to immediately alert authorities that a threat to humanity has appeared in your dining room and asked for second helpings of mashed potatoes. Helping your children grow into strong, confident adults is much more difficult if their home world has been reduced to rubble by alien invaders. The one exception may actually be the daleks: in their case, a mysterious traveler called "The Doctor" (even though nobody has ever seen a degree from an accredited medical school with his name on it) usually appears to save the day.

Oh, and, babe, since I have you here, I gotta ask: what's the point of asking me for help **after** you've kicked your daughter out of the house? Talk about closing the barn door after the genetically re-emergent mastadon has escaped! Not much I can do now – your daughter is probably being fitted with a plunger nose even as we speak!

Send your relationship problems to the Alternate Reality News Service's *sex, love and technology columnist at questions@lespagesauxfolles.ca. Amritsar Al-Falloudjianapour is not a trained therapist, but she does know a lot of stuff. AMRITSAR SAYS: I cannot stress enough how good an idea it is to submit your question to me BEFORE you take irreversible action. I'm here to help, not to judge. But, in my judgment, I can't help you if you don't help me. Deal? Deal.*

Ask Amritsar: How Can We Miss You, If...

Dear Amritsar,

Towards the end of his life, my grandpa Bluttmange (yeah, that's his real name – he's from Moosejaw) was not the nicest person. He used to hide his dentures in among the feminine hygiene products of the women who lived in the Raymondo Dentrifice Home for the Aged and Terminally Short of Cash; when he was caught, he claimed he thought he was putting them in a glass of water...a square glass of water that wasn't wet but did contain a lot of spray cans.

When people at the Home pointed out that the day before the dentures incident he had written in his diary, "Gonna play a trick on some uptight beyotches today," Grandpa Bluttmange claimed that chipmunks had stolen his diary and forged entries in it as revenge for his favouring the pigeons when he tossed bread crumbs to the animals during "nature time." He kept to this story even when it was pointed out that the there were no chipmunks within a 50 metre radius of the Home.

"What, you got sonar or something?" Grandpa Bluttmange groused. Actually, the Home does, but the residents who are protected by it aren't supposed to know that, so this confrontation ended in a stalemate.

Then, there was the incident with the atomic cheese grater, the stewardesses and the ternary Goldbach conjecture. You...uhh, you may remember seeing that one on CNN.

As bad as he was in life, Grandpa Bluttmange has been worse since he died.

The salesman at the Kamikaze Cemetery (he told us that the word meant "happy happy joy joy beyond life life") convinced us to get Grandpa Bluttmange's mind scanned just before he died. The scan was then put on a chip which

animates his face on a screen built into his tombstone. When we visit the gravesite, it's like being with him again. Nobody in the family can really articulate why that's supposed to be a good thing.

Within a week, Grandpa Bluttmange's headstone had convinced the headstone of Erma Mae Woodpecker that her family didn't love her because they hadn't buried her in the shade of a tree, and that it was only a matter of time before the weather deteriorated her computer scan to the point where she was a gibbering wreck. They're headstones, for goodness' sake! They're made of granite! They'll be around long after global warming has forced humanity to find somewhere else to live!

I'd like to hear Grandpa Bluttmange complain about how infrequently we visit after *that* happens!

Then, when I took my 10 year-old son, Theosophilus, to see Grandpa Bluttmange's memorial, the old man told him, "Do yourself a favour and kill yourself now. Life is all downhill from here, kid." Now, arguably, that's true. Still, it wasn't appropriate. It didn't help that he added: "Course, even death ain't permanent, now. If you kill yourself in a fire, there's a good chance they won't be able to recreate your consciousness. Wanna know where your dad keeps his lighter?" Needless to say, Osoph was traumatized; I don't like the way he has looked at matches ever since.

So, what I want to know is this: if I set off an electromagnetic pulse in the vicinity of Grandpa Bluttmange's memorial, would frying his computer chip be like murdering him?

[name withheld pending explication of the legal ramifications of the answer to the question]

Hey, Babe,

We like to think that we want to remember our deceased loved ones as they were after they have passed on. However, unless they were Mother Teresa or Superman, there are usually aspects of them that we would rather bury deeper than nuclear waste. Not only that, but we would happily vote on enough appropriations to actually keep them safely stored there for the next 10,000 years.

Under ordinary circumstances, all we have to go on are our memories of our loved ones, and memories are as solid as guacamole in a hurricane. Unless, I suppose, the guacamole's atomic lattices had been rigidified with hypercooling processes, but, in that case, I wouldn't want to dip my nachos in it on Saturday night.

The problem with projecting your loved ones on their tombstones is that, like the guest who eats all of your nachos on Saturday night, their continued presence doesn't give you the chance to grieve their death. This leaves you in a limbo that keeps you from getting on with your life, and that's a bar that will never get high enough for you to dance under.

So, I say fry the bastard.

Send your relationship problems to the Alternate Reality News Service's *sex, love and technology columnist at questions@lespagesauxfolles.ca. Amritsar Al-Falloudjianapour is not a trained therapist, but she does know a lot of stuff. AMRITSAR SAYS: what do I look like, a lawyer? Although, judge's robes are so slimming...*

Ask The Tech Answer Guy for Zombie Clarification

Yo, Tech Answer Guy,

I recently discovered that somebody is using my Granny Stilton's Visa Unobtainium card. Yeah, yeah, I know that the Unobtainium card has a half-life of 17 million years, but Granny Stilton doesn't: she perished in the invasion of the malevolent garden gnomes from Earth Prime 3-8-7-7-0-1 dash omicron two years ago. Or, so we thought. How can I tell if the credit card is being used by an identity thief or by my grandmother returned to walk the earth as a zombie?

Sincerely,
Molloch from Gomorrah

Yo, Molly,

You're in luck. The Centres for Zombie Control and Digital Crime Eradication (which was voted runner-up in *Forbes* magazine's July poll of Least Believable Government Agency Names) just released a Consumer Alert on this very subject. Their advice on how to tell the difference between zombie relatives and identity thieves includes:

- A thief will try to evade your grasp for as long as possible; whether or not it succeeds will depend on the quality of local law enforcement. A zombie will try to get you in its grasp as soon as possible; whether or not it succeeds will depend on how fast you can run.

- If the credit card is being used to buy a vacation on the Riviera, you should probably put your lawyer on speed dial. If it is being used to buy headcheese, you should probably get out the shotgun.

- Zombies are little bit country. Identity thieves are a little bit rock and roll.

- If their high school yearbook reads: "MOST LIKELY TO: travel the world under assumed names," you've probably got a case of identity theft. If their high school yearbook reads: MOST LIKELY TO: dribble disgusting liquids on you on your first date," you've probably got a textbook example of a zombie.

- Have you noticed people coming to repossess your car, cat or catamaran? Then, you're probably dealing with an identity thief. Have you noticed diseased body parts appearing on the lawns in your neighbourhood? Then, you're probably dealing with a zombie apocalypse. Make sure you have plenty of ammo for your shotgun.

- An identity thief will want to keep its own identity a secret for as long as possible. To a zombie, the concept of personal identity is a secret.

- Zombies tend to vote Republican. Identity thieves tend to vote Libertarian.

- Identity thieves usually wear designer clothes from Ralph Lauren or Junya Watanabe. Zombies sport the latest rotting clothes look from Toby's House of Advancing Decrepitude.

- Identity thieves want your money. Zombies want your blood. No, wait – that's vampires. Sorry for the confusion.

- If its Twitter description reads, "Credit cards are like potato chips – you can't stop at just one!", you're probably dealing with an identity thief. If its Twitter description reads, "aaauuungh rowf browf aaaaaaaargluuuuuung!", you're probably dealing with a zombie (although there is a slight chance that you are dealing with an identity thief who fell asleep at its keyboard).

- After they die, zombies can be found in the level of hell that includes butchers whose thumbs stray onto their scales, people who post messages on their Farcebook pages that are ALL IN CAPS and people who let their four year-old children watch Three Stooges movies. After they die, identity thieves can be found in the level of hell that includes movie reviewers who don't warn you about spoilers, politicians who don't warn you that you will be rewarded for your vote for them by the gutting of programmes you rely on and potential boyfriends who don't warn you that they've been Three Stooges fans since they were four. Of course, this knowledge won't help you until after **you** die, but if you're the sort of person who has an insatiable curiosity, it is good to know.

- If the person uses the credit card to get a subscription to *Cryptkeepers Monthly*, it's probably a zombie. If the person gets a subscription to *The New York*

Review of Books, it's probably an identity thief, and a well read identity thief at that.

- If the perpetrator's ring tone is a song by The Hooters called "All You Zombies" or anything by Dead Can Dance…it doesn't really prove anything. The identity thief could just be a fan.

- If you live in a Dean Koontz novel, your grannie is probably a zombie. If you live in a Robert J. Sawyer novel, her credit card is probably being used by an identity thief.

Of course, there is always the possibility that the identity thief is a zombie. If you suspect that that is the case, look for next month's Centres for Zombie Control and Digital Crime Eradication (voted the fourth worst dressed government agency in a *Tiger Beat* poll)'s guidelines for how to deal with that situation.

The Tech Answer Guy

If you are a dude with a question about the latest technology, ask The Tech Answer Guy by sending it to questions@lespagesauxfolles.ca. Just remember: never dip your tie in the finger bowl after May 1. Dip it into the shrimp sauce, instead.

Ask Amritsar About Video Fame

Dear Amritsar,

When I was two years old, I pulled the tail of the family cat, Rosicrucian Index. I'm not sure what made me do it – I was just improvising, I guess. Well! Old Rosidex' eyes bugged out of its skull like it was in a cartoon, and it howled in surprise. At least, my parents told me it was a howl of surprise.

My parents, Bob and Esther, were videotaping my interactions with the cat. Either they wanted a heartwarming testament to my childhood or they were involved in some bizarre psych experiment that they wanted to write a groundbreaking journal paper about. Or, both. Motivation is not important, here. The important thing is that they put the video on YouTube, where it got 1.347 million views in 24 hours. One point three four seven! In the next two months, my video, "Cat on a Hot Tin Ruth," would go on to be seen over 10 million times.

I was a star!

And, like any child star, I had the problem of how to top a phenomenal success at such a young age. It took a couple of months, but my opportunity arose at my third birthday party. I was being held up by my 92 year-old great-grandma Conssumpcion, when I felt a gurgling in my tummy. I was tempted to spew my curdled bananas and broccoli all over her, but, even then, I had a sense that my audience wasn't into full-on gross-out humour, so, instead, I burped loudly in her face.

"Ruth and Consequences" racked up a respectable 500,000 views on YouTube over the next six months, but respectable was no longer good enough for me. Over the next year and a half, I tried everything I could think of to regain my audience: falling on my face, taking a tablecloth with me and pulling all the plates and glasses on the table down on me;

repeating the word "POOP!" over and over again for 36 hours in as many different ways as I could think of; smearing actual poop on the cat (this episode was considered "too controversial" and was never aired); all of the artistic tools at the disposal of somebody still in diapers. Nothing was too degrading for me to do to try and find my audience.

But, no matter what I did, my numbers declined drastically.

I tried putting a block of wood with the letter Q painted on the side up my nose, but it barely got 1,000 views. I guess my audience wasn't ready for a conceptual piece. (By the way, the screams on the video were real; I had to be taken to the hospital to get the block removed. If you thought the slow-down-to-get-a-glimpse-of-the accident crowd were interested in watching an artist suffer for her art, well, you can just forget it!)

In the wake of the wooden block fiasco, I decided to take a break from my artistic career. To be honest, eating, pooping and napping – especially napping – took up most of my time and creative attention in any case.

When I returned to the stage a couple of months later, I thought I would give the audience an old favourite: I pulled Rosidex' tail again. Twice. This gave my popularity a bit of a spike, peaking at 10,498 views, but, obviously the time for that act had passed.

Am I washed up at the age of four?

Ruth

Hey, Babe,

You seem awfully media savvy for somebody who is so young. Obviously, the person who said, "They're getting younger every year" didn't know the half of it!

As it happens, I saw "Cat on a Hot Tin Ruth" when it first came out. I remember thinking: *Wow. And, we thought television was dumbing down the masses!*

You want my honest opinion? The entertainment world already has enough monsters – I'm not about to encourage another one. Do everybody a favour and take up another career, one more appropriate to your age – have you considered walking or language acquisition?

Send your relationship problems to the Alternate Reality News Service's *sex, love and technology columnist at questions@lespagesauxfolles.ca. Amritsar Al-Falloudjianapour is not a trained therapist, but she does know a lot of stuff. AMRITSAR SAYS: you know how you posted a message to saw.you.at.com about that gorgeous person you saw briefly in the cafeteria/strip club/church basement hoping to connect with her or him?* **Why didn't you just go up to the person and introduce yourself to him or her when you had the chance?**

Ask The Tech Answer Guy
About the Shelf Elf™ From Hell

Yo, Tech Answer Guy,

When I was growing up, people had some strange ideas about parenting. Remember the Three in the Morning Movement, where parents blared The Smiths in the middle of the night to show their infant children how it felt to be woken up by loud, petulant whining? That lasted long enough for an entire generation to grow up sleep deprived and cranky! And, of course, the less said about The Gluterberg Cavebaby Diet, the better.

Not to be outdone, when I was four, my parents got me a Shelf Elf™.

It's a bland looking plush doll, with long, loose limbs, a soft, expressionless face, pointy ears and a red cap. You wouldn't think, to look at it as an adult, that it was all that scary, but bland contains its own special kind of menace, don't you think? I certainly think. That, I mean. About the menace.

My parents told me that it would watch me and relay my behaviour back to Santa Claus; the Shelf Elf™'s reports would determine if I would get on the Naughty or Nice list. Big Elf was watching my every move! Room 101 was the corner I was sent to when I acted up! My god, I was taught good and evil before I could even pronounce Nietche! I mean, Nitsche! I mean – oh, you know who I mean!

Of course, when I was old enough to know the difference between good watching over and evil surveillance (some time in the first semester of my second year of university), I decided to put the Shelf Elf™ away. I graduated, got a job, married and had a couple of kids of my own – all that boring adult stuff. I thought that part of my life was over. More fool me.

After a particularly nasty argument with Deirdtree – that's my wife – about who should be responsible for filling the garbage vaporizer, I noticed that the Shelf Elf™ appeared on the dresser across from our bed. Not a problem – I put it back in its box in the back of my wife's moderately naughty lingerie closet and didn't give it a second thought. Then, it appeared after we fought about who should tell our eldest daughter, Wilhelmina, that she couldn't go to the Saidye Bronfman's dance wearing **that** outfit!

The more we fought, the more the Shelf Elf™ appeared. Seeing the demon doll in such emotionally trying circumstances brought back the old fear; it got so bad that I started agreeing with whatever Deirdtree wanted just to keep from having to see it again!

I've done everything I could to make the Shelf Elf™ go away. I stabbed it. I shot it. I took it a mile outside the city limits and left it by the side of the road. I pulled it apart and buried the parts in various backyards around the nieghbourhood. I pureed it and sprinkled it on my morning eggs. (Don't do that – it makes breakfast taste funny.) Yet, no matter what I did to the Shelf Elf™, it always turned up the next time I had a fight with Deirdtree.

What's happening to me?

Sincerely,
Igor from Innisfil

Yo, Iggy,

Man up! It's just a lifeless doll! What? You think you're Karen Black in some cheap 1970s horror movie? If so, you're beyond my help – get an exorcist. Or, a film critic. Roger Ebert is the best, but he does so many Blackorcisms that you have to book him years in advance. A. O. Scott is a bit of a Karen Black heretic, but his demon doll removal technique is impeccable, so he will do in a pinch.

Are you all manly and shit now? Good. Then, follow the asterisk at the end of this paragraph. Yo, guys – the asterisk is just for Iggy, okay? Everybody else can take a powder (which does not mean have a donut, although, now that you mention it, that's not a bad idea, especially if it will get us some privacy). Capisce? (Which does mean put a cap on your isce, good advice in these times of antibiotic- and rational argument-resistant STDs.) Good.*

The Tech Answer Guy

* Heeeey! What'd I say? Following the asterisk is just for Iggy! Yeah, I'm looking at you, Ignatowski! Think you can get in on this passage on a technicality? Gimme a break! Seriously. I'll see you next time. This is just for one reader.

Are we alone? Good. I had a Shelf Elf™ when I was a kid, Iggy, and I don't mind admitting to just you that it scared the bejesus out of me! (Bejesus, as you may know, is a form of ectoplasm that exists west of the Mason-Dixon line). To this day, I cannot watch *The Santa Clause* without breaking into a sweat!

You say the Shelf Elf™ appears every time you have a fight with your wife? And, its presence makes you afraid to fight with her? What's going on is obvious: your wife's lover comes into your home in the middle of the night and places a new Shelf Elf™ in your bedroom! I guess he figures that if he drives you mad, it will give your wife an excuse to divorce you, allowing her to be with him.

Bastard.

The solution is to figure out which of your neighbours is cuckolding (literally: making you an old cuck) you, find his weakness and then steal into his house and plant a representation of said weakness there for him to find. (When in doubt, a horse's head has been shown to work in 19 out of 20 screenings of *The Godfather*). You will find that taking action to end your torment will stem the fear that eats away at your soul (leeching it of vital Omega 3s).

Revenge, as they say, is a dish best served cold-cocked!

If you are a dude with a question about the latest technology, ask The Tech Answer Guy by sending it to questions@lespagesauxfolles.ca. Just remember: what doesn't kill you makes your need for a lifetime of therapy stronger!

Ask Amritsar: Holiday Dinners App-en

Dear Amritsar,

You know what would increase my holiday spirit, other than spiking the egg nog with clam chowder? Is there any technology for helping me deal with obnoxious family members at holiday dinners?

Babette Brewster

Hey, Babe,

Is there? Does Santa poop in Padua? (The answer, in case you don't have access to his flight itinerary, is yes: he also makes stops for bathroom breaks in Inuvik, Sydney and Chichicastenango.) Here is a small sampling of the holiday season's most useful cellphone apps:

Tired of hearing that toilet paper was softer and finishing the *New York Times* Jumble puzzle was harder when your grandfather was a wee spratling? Then, an app called I Don't Wanna Hear It, Grandpa! (Plunkman and Progeny Coding, $2.99) is just for you. Enter the claim and the approximate date, and the app will find anywhere from four to a dozen things that were worse then than they are today. Imagine the satisfaction you'll get when you're able to say, "Actually, gramps, golf may have been golfier when you were a kid, but 2,746 people died when the USS Tempting Fate hit an iceberg lettuce and sank without a trace!"

One of the...special joys of the holidays is having to endure questions from your mother about why you aren't currently seeing anyone and when you think you could maybe you know settle down and get married and okay, okay, I know I'm being a little pushy but, really, a person could grow old waiting for grandchildren! Sound familiar? If so, you'll want to get Yenta Relentah (Izikoff International Duckies, $3.99). This app creates a fictional boyfriend for you, complete with images, full personal history and credit rating! You'll be the envy of your mother's Mahjong group in no time!

Did you grow up with a sister who everybody thought was prettier than you were? If so, you might want to get the Full Facial Nudity app (Sibling Revelry, $1.99). It shortens your sister's eyelashes, removes her lipstick, changes her hair to a mousy brown and gives her ugly glasses and earrings. If, after all this, she still looks better than you do, apply the Ugly Duckling extension (Green-eyed Monster, Inc., $0.99); this will puff up her face (no more perfect cheekbones!), thin her lips and give her bags around her eyes. Think of the pleasure you'll get posting **that** image to your Farcebook page!

Trim the Twins (Ink Link for Linc, Inc., $5.99) is the perfect app to deal with bratty children at the holiday dinner table. Based on the book *Battle Scenes of the 20th Century*, it contains over 200 images of war carnage; although it was originally intended for history buffs, it can quell the enthusiasm of even the naughtiest children at 50 paces! Unless your family name is Adams, in which case an app that features images of adorable kittens should have the same effect.

Do you have an Uncle Kenny? You know the one we mean – the guy who is constantly telling everybody at the turkey table about how great his car/virtual reality rig/robot yacht/trophy wife/life is? Of course you do. Everybody has an Uncle Kenny (or Steve or Philboyd or Terr duc Ken). So, everybody could use the Silence is Golden app (Farrelly Brothers, $4.99). At any point in one of Uncle Kenny's egomaniacal monologues, simply click on the Start button and SHOVE YOUR CELLPHONE DOWN HIS THROAT! Silence is Golden will beep when you have reached the perfect

depth, the one where the flow of self-satisfaction stops but no permanent damage is done to your phone.

Merry Christmas! Happy Hanukkah! [INSERT APPROPRIATE ADJECTIVE HERE] Kwanzaa! And, for my atheist friends, enjoy making fun of and feeling superior to everybody else!

Dear Amritsar,

What if I can't recognize anybody in

Babette Brewster

Hey, Babe...tte,

What if you can't recognize anybody in your family in the apps I have described? Would you believe: THERE'S AN APP FOR THAT! Just type details of the relative you are having problems with into the Hell is Other People at Family Holiday Dinners app (Sommelier Sartre, $19.99), and it will search the thousands of family-related apps available on the Internet for just the one you need! It's a little pricey, but, really, how can anybody put a price on holiday cheer?

Dear Amritsar,

You're the best! Thanks!

Babette Brewster

Hey, Babe,

No need to thank me. It's what I do.

Send your relationship problems to the Alternate Reality News Service's *sex, love and technology columnist at questions@lespagesauxfolles.ca. Amritsar Al-Falloudjianapour is not a trained therapist, but she does know a lot of stuff. AMRITSAR SAYS: if you look around the table and you're the only one who isn't furiously typing on their cellphone, the problem is you. To be safe, wear a bib...*

Ask The Tech Answer Guy About Familial Obligations

Yo, Tech Answer Guy,

My great-grandfather Izzy's knees are going out. Again. Family legend has it that this is the 20th set, and, thanks to the laws of diminishing returns, it only took them three hours after surgery before they started creaking and oozing disgusting liquids.

Thanks, law of diminishing returns.

Meanwhile, my great-grandmother Sammie's neural interface is getting glitchier by the second, making it harder and harder for her to access her memories in the cloud. She can remember playing MC5 records on something called a stereo as if it was yesterday, even though electricity has been

strictly rationed for over 800 years. Interns at the Methuselah Rest Home and Soil Reclamation Factory say she's going to Cloud Cuckoo Land, like I don't know what they're talking about, like it's that hard to figure out what they mean, like I care what they think.

Everybody in the family says I should go to the Home every day and drain Izzy's knees (eww!) and comfort Sammie (double eww with carob chocolate sauce!). I'm only 15! I was looking forward to downloading a degree in MacroWikinomics directly into my neural network and spending my life teaching advanced civilizations in Polynesia the economic advantages of macrame. Instead, I can look forward to a future of looking after my great-grandparents.

Like I like it.

Everybody else in my family seems to have an excuse to get out of great-grandparent duty. My parents, Fromp and Adena, lost everything in the Furian Chewing Gum bubble and are surviving on virtual food stamps. My grandparents, Harold, Maude and Voicebox1, are vacationing on Mars and are not answering their phones. My great-grandparents, Pat and Other Pat, are useless because they had shells grafted onto their bodies and no longer have opposable thumbs. It's turtles and excuses all the way down.

This is unfair! Izzy and Sammie have 537 great-grandchildren; why can't we all share looking after our great-grandparents? If we did, we would each only have to see our great-grandparents once every year and a half or so!

Can you think of a way I can stick my cousin, 23 times removed, RebeCCah with this onerous family duty?

Sincerely,
@n1ta from Argentina

Yo, Nita,

Intergenerational conflicts take on a whole new meaning when people can live to be 1,000, don't they?

Like Xeno's Retirement Age Paradox, with the average retirement being pushed further and further into people's lives. Freedom 500 – it has a ring to it, don't you think? Naah – me neither. Still, aside from forestalling the inevitable, it guarantees that people of the 3399FF Generation remain blue because they can't find any jobs.

Of course, it gets worse. In order to make room on the planet for all these coddled codgers, these gentrified geriatrics, these obscene oldsters, most governments of advanced nations – and France – now have a quarter child policy, where only every fourth couple can have a baby. Solomon would have a seizure!

My suggestion to you would be to stow away on a cargo ship to the Oort Cloud and hope that when you get there they'll take pity on you and let you work in the Virgin Helium Mines.

The Tech Answer Guy

Yo, Tech Answer Guy,

How sharper than a serpent's tooth it is to have a thankless great-grandchild!

You should not be encouraging @n1ta from Argentina to shirk her duty to look after her great-grandparents! I'm 667 years old, and still a productive member of society. Every other Thursday and twice on Sundays. When my prosthetic spleen isn't acting up (it does like its Beckett in the Park...ing Lot). When my neural network reminds me.

Well. My personal details are probably only of interest to rogue demographers and freelance daisy painters. My point is that @n1ta from Argentina's great-grandparents made this world what it is today. Without them, her great-grandparents wouldn't exist. Without **them**, her great-great-great-great-great-great-great-great-great-great-great-

great-grandparents would never have been born. Without them – well, I think you get my point.

Children like @n1ta from Argentina should respect their elders. After all, they haven't been where we've been, but we've been where they've been. Even if we can't quite put our fingers on the memory's address in the cloud.

Sincerely,
T1na from La Isla Bonita

Yo, Teens,

You clearly don't remember what it's like to be young and carefree and have your own teeth. If you watched more coming of age holovids, you might not feel the way you do. Or, you might, but you'd be so busy watching coming of age holovids that you wouldn't have the time to express those feelings. I'd be good with it either way.

The Tech Answer Guy

If you are a dude with a question about the latest technology, ask The Tech Answer Guy by sending it to questions@lespagesauxfolles.ca. Just remember: old people are icky. Thousand year-old people are icky to the power of yuck.

Ask The Tech Answer Guy: Something Fishy Going On

Yo, Tech Answer Guy,

My mate and I had high hopes for our eldest offspring, Blurble 238,976. As a young scrod, he loved to play with the other fish – we were sure his popularity would win him many mates who would honour us with schoolsful of grandchildren.

Unfortunately, in adolescence, Blurble 238,976 has grown sullen and distant. He rarely swims with his friends – most of the time he flops around on the not-water, breathing. Breathing! Our little Blurble 238,976! You never think it will happen to one of your own children, but, as we now know, you never know.

Breathing! It's a disgusting habit which I understand can be very addictive. (I tried it once myself when I was younger, but I didn't inhale.) We have tried to talk to Blurble 238,976 about it, but he always denies that there is anything wrong. One time, we tried to set up an intervention for him, but when he realized what was happening, he quickly swam into a coral reef and refused to come out until we agreed to stop it.

Is there anything we can do to keep our son from being destroyed by this terrible habit?

Sincerely,
Blurble 238,974 from the Baltic

Yo, Blurbs,

I wouldn't worry about it too much. Children always act out, but, as they get older, they invariably become better behaved. I expect that young Blurble 238,976 will grow out of this phase. That, or, a millennium or two from now, he will have evolved into the banker who destroys the world economy through the use of computer trading and derivatives.

It's all good.

The Tech Answer Guy

Yo, Tech Answer Guy,

I wrote to the Ask Amritsar column in this publication about my passionately held belief that cosplay – where…girls dress up in costumes – is killing science fiction fandom. Sure, guys Live Action Role Play, but that's completely different! LARPers in costumes actually do things! Things like running around and hitting each other with foam swords! Cosplayers just stand around and talk about Japanese cartoons that I've never heard of. Once in a while, they strike a pose, but how can that possibly compare to running around and hitting people with foam swords?

It can't. That's how.

Costume play really brings down the intellectual level of science fiction fandom. It is an activity for seven year-olds. Okay, LARPing is an activity for 12 year-olds. Still, those five years are fundamental to the intellectual growth of a child, so I trust my point is clear.

Instead of complimenting me on my perspicuity, Amritsar lectured me on how different forms of fandom are equally legitimate; she obviously feels very passionate about this subject, as her column filled four full pages. Towards the end, she called me vile names, terrible names, names that I didn't think you could say in a family publication. Especially not in the original Klingon!

Still, I'm right, aren't I? Cosplay is just a feminized, diminished form of fandom. Right?

Sincerely,
Morton Montmorency from Muncie

Yo, Mort,

Are you advice column shopping? Really? That's just ugly, man. I bet Dear Abby never had to put up with that shit.

Over the years, The Tech Answer Guy has compiled a list of Things You Must Never Do. You don't trod on Superman's cape. You don't spit into the wind. You don't pull that mask off the old Lone – okay, you know what? You're right if you noticed that this is actually Jim Croce's list of Things You Must Never Do. I…I seem to have left my list of Things You Must Never Do in my other pair of pants (which is, of course, a Porsche).

The important thing is that I never, never, never stick my wicket in Amritsar's face! Call it professional courtesy. Call it primal fear. Either way, I don't sashay all over Amritsar's drapes. I don't make google-eyes at Amritsar's perfume cabinet. I don't get all up in her schnitzel, fo' shitzel. Uhh…dog. Are you getting the gist of my nub? I'm saying that I never poke my nub where it isn't welcome, and Amritsar's baking soda is one of those places!

If you've got a beef with the advice Amritsar Al-Falloudjianapour has given you, take it anyway. Trust me, it's easier for everybody that way.

The Tech Answer Guy

If you are a dude with a question about the latest technology, ask The Tech Answer Guy by sending it to questions@lespagesauxfolles.ca. Just remember: Amritsar packs a mean punch for such a tiny scrawny woman. I mean, her left hook could fell an ox! Trust me on this – you'd be better off messing around with Jim!

Ask Amritsar About The Talk

Dear Amritsar,

My dad is 37 and my mom is 34. Should I have The Talk with them now, or have I left it too late?

Timmy (aged 12)

Hey, Babe,

Parents can be so difficult, sometimes, can't they?

Family therapists and cardboard cutouts of 18th century world leaders cannot seem to agree on when the best time for The Talk is. Some argue that, given the accelerating pace of technological change in the world, 30 year-old parents may already be too clueless to understand the environment in which their children live. A different some (possibly arrived at using a different numerical base) argue that unbelievably old parents, maybe even 40, could appreciate some aspects of The Talk, even if they are likely to miss some of the subtle nuances.

Everybody generally agrees, though, that the sooner you have The Talk, the better. The cardboard cutout of France's Henry IV is especially adamant on this point.

When you first try to initiate The Talk with one or both of your parents, look for subtle clues that they are able to comprehend what you are saying. If, for instance, you try to explain to your father where Tweets come from, and he puts his hands over his ears and starts shouting, "Ooh, get away from me! Cooties! COOTIES!", you've probably left it too long. Similarly, if your mother hugs her knees, rocks back and forth and moans, "I never knew. I never knew. I never knew," over and over again, it's probably too late to give her The Talk.

Some adults are so scared by The Talk that they will insist that they want to have their own The Talk with you. DO NOT FALL FOR THIS! THIS IS A DIVERSIONARY TACTIC TO AVOID DEALING WITH AN UNCOMFORTABLE TRUTH! In the face of resistance, calmly but firmly assert the primacy of your concerns, reassuring them that it's natural for children to have a different relationship to technology than their parents, especially as the speed of change increases. At first, they may be overwhelmed by what you are trying to tell them; it never hurts to have an episode of *Murder, She Wrote* or *Golden Girls* cued up and ready to go in case they need to be calmed down.

Patience is the key to a successful The Talk, especially if your parents initially resist what you're trying to tell them. If, at first, The Talk does not go well, as tempted as you may be in your frustration, do not start a Twitter account called "Shit My Dad Says." This will likely embarrass your parents. And, it will definitely get you sued by William Shatner. Celebrity lawsuits are never good for family harmony.

Despite all of the potential problems, it's important to have The Talk with your parents, because tech information they get from the streets may be unreliable. Your parents might try to buy a cam peripheral from a shady dealer at the back of a Best Buy, but, when they get it home, you find that they have actually bought a penguin. Good luck trying to find the person who sold it to them, let alone get reimbursed for all of the pickled herring your family has to buy while waiting to hear if the local zoo is willing to take the penguin off your hands!

The problem may not be so obvious, though. If you ask them in a non-judging way, your parents may open up and admit that they have experimented with Pinterest. There is nothing wrong with this, per se; parents are naturally inquisitive, and will try out new technologies without a real sense of the consequences. The whole point of The Talk is to make sure that they are made aware of the consequences, so that when they are ready to use the latest technologies, they do so as safely as possible.

However it goes, always keep in mind that you love your parents very much and want what's least embarrassing for them. Oh, and that your children will someday have to give you The Talk. Most children seem to forget this fact. I would recommend tattooing it on your chest.

Send your relationship problems to the Alternate Reality News Service's *sex, love and technology columnist at questions@lespagesauxfolles.ca.* Amritsar Al-Falloudjianapour *is not a trained therapist, but she does know a lot of stuff. AMRITSAR SAYS: you know how, wearing Google glasses, people of the opposite sex are willing to forgive you for walking into them because they assume that you didn't quite see them there? That excuse for feeling others up is only going to work for early adopters, and not for very long. When more people have experience with Google glasses, they are going to learn that they contain anti-collision software (combining GPS tracking, echolocation and the Colonel's secret recipe of eleven herbs and spices) that warns users when they are getting too close to another object. Perv.*

Ask Amritsar About Technology-Crost Lovers

Dear Amritsar,

My love for Rom-3-0 burns stronger than a thousand supernovas. I love him more than – wait, that isn't right. A supernova is an exploding star that can incinerate entire solar systems. Cosmic debris is not romantic. Let me try again.

My love for Rom-3-0 binds us more strongly than the weak nuclear force. Okay, the name may not sound like much, but it's the force that is responsible for the decay of atomic particles, one of the four fundamental forces of nature, so you know that it's an important part of making the universe what it – oh, crap!

Look, my difficulty with metaphors notwithstanding, I love the big lug, okay?

All of my friends in the Lemming Mind have seen us exchange spit (held in ceremonial moccasins with our names engraved in obsolete computer chips on the side – we're not barbarians, you know!). They were thrilled when he started writing love poems to me, and they were ecstatic when he stopped.

The problem with our relationship can be summed up in a question I often ask him: Rom-3-0, Rom-3-0, wherefore port thou Rom-3-0?

Put another, perhaps less cryptic but definitely not as poetic way, the day I was born, a Fredrickson was implanted in my brain that would allow me to plug into computers through a fingertip interface and even access wireless local area networks. Rom-3-0's family couldn't afford a Fredrickson, and he has grown up deprived.

I don't care! Really, I don't! Okay, when we're making out, my digitally-enhanced senses can hear his heart beating faster than a Stanchurian Velocipede AND I can smell the increase in pheromones and various chemicals in his body AND I can ask for advice from my male friends in the Lemming Mind to ensure that I give Rom-3-0 the maximum amount of pleasure. Meanwhile, he gropes around like a demented ape child.

I. Don't. Care. Rom-3-0 is sweet and kind and really knows how to fill out a spandex gherkin. How could I not love him?

Unfortunately, my family has been beastly about the relationship. And, I don't mean they project the images of wolves and cheetahs and pandas (Grandpa Strumpet is easily confused) onto my retinas whenever I try to talk about him. Well, not just that. I mean, they forbid me from seeing Rom-3-0, in normal, ultraviolet or any other spectrum of light!

His parents have been no better. They say things to him like, "You know that everybody in her Lemming Hive sees everything that goes on between you, don't you? It's like living in the 1960s, but without the exquisite fashions!" And, "You realize that as you get older, your memory will fade but hers will get stronger, don't you? After you turn 50, kiss any possibility of winning an argument goodbye!" And, "Does her Frederickson get cable?" So far, Rom-3-0's love for me hasn't wavered, although he did express curiosity about the cable thing.

O, Amritsar, O, Amritsar, my situation is hopeless, by far. Should we run away, or should we kill ourselves before the end of day?

Jul-1-3-t

Hey, Babe,

Tough one.

I asked my good friend Deepak Chopra about your dilemma, but he told me he would be busy getting his cuticles enlarged (oh, the vanity of men!) and he wouldn't be available for several months. Perhaps having heard that I was seeking help for your problem, my goodish friend Oprah stopped returning my calls, and she has never done that before, even during the Twine Flu epidemic. My okay but with the potential to be a good friend some day Tony Robbins claimed that he was actually Tim Robbins, and insisted he couldn't help me because he was fighting with Susan Sarandon. Phil, the mechanic from the shop down the street, said this was the Landau's Problems of relationships; I should have known better than to trust a good friend of The Tech Answer Guy!

Really tough one.

So. It's down to me. Why am I not surprised? (Actually, I had my surprise glands removed when I was a child, but that knowledge in no way helps you, so forget I answered.)

Many things – skin colour, religion, walls – separate people. Love is the subcutaneous laser scalpel that can cut through the cancer of hate and leave you with an adorable scar on your belly. By all means, run away and try to make your relationship work. On the other hand, you will have to cut yourself off from the Lemming Mind, or else your parents will see every detail of your relationship; if you killed yourself now, you would save everybody a lot of Shakespearean melodrama.

Am I being indecisive? Sorry – I suddenly find I need to get my cuticles enlarged!

Send your relationship problems to the Alternate Reality News Service's *sex, love and technology columnist at questions@lespagesauxfolles.ca. Amritsar Al-Falloudjianapour is not a trained therapist, but she does know a lot of stuff. AMRITSAR SAYS: it's just a coincidence that my responses to the questions of readers are precisely long enough to fill my word count, and nobody can prove otherwise!*

Ask The Tech Answer Guy About the Sound of Music

Yo, Tech Answer Guy,

Every Saint Safron Foer Day, my gramps Kareem is taken out of cryogenic stasis to eat traditional holiday fare like pumpkin bagels with smoked alfalfa sprouts and, of course, heart of musk ox in a hollandaise drip, and to tell us how much better life was when he was our age. You know what I'm talking about.

Shaving was so much better in the old days because you had a real feel for it when you had to do it by hand. It wasn't like today, when you can genetically tweak your facial hair to be any length you want it to be (or quickly grow and cut itself at random intervals, all the rage in clubs these days).

Kids today got it easy. Wrestling carp was much better way back when because they didn't have iCarpFishing apps for their prosthetic limbs.

And, don't even ask about communications! Back in the Dark Ages of Gramps' youth, they actually had to etch their messages in stone tablets before their computer email programmes would send them!

This year, I made the mistake of listening to my pPod at the dinner table. I thought I could drown Gramps out, but he just shouted, "Oh, yeah. In my day, music was better than that crap the young people listen to today!"

Is there any research that would prove that my Gramps is wrong about today's music? Because, you know, I would love an excuse to argue that he should be left in cryogenic stasis until I'm older than he is so I could outrank him in the Things Were Better When I Was Young Sweepstakes!

Sincerely,
Kelvin Klamato from Dartmouth

Yo, Kelv,

I got good news and I got bad news. The good news is that there is research about the quality of popular music over time. The bad news is that it supports your grandfather's claim that music was better when he was young.

Joan Serra and her team at the Spanish National Research Council (which sounds like something some crazed satirist made up – right? – but really does exist) built an artificial intelligence that analyzed all of the popular music produced over the last 50 years. They called the programme Streep Thought, after the actress/inventor of the nuclear powered Q-Tip – sorry, cotton swab[not TM].

When they asked Streep Thought if music was getting better or worse, the programme responded, "Difficult." Then, 37 seconds later, it answered, "Worse." When asked about its initial reaction, Streep Thought shrugged and replied, "I was trying to inject a little drama into the proceedings."

"We obtained numerical indicators," explained Serra, "that the diversity of transitions between note combinations – roughly speaking chords plus melodies plus sitar solos – has consistently diminished in the last 50 years."

Serra's findings support the Third Dunkin Donuts Hypothesis, which states that: "As corporate control over the music industry consolidates, all popular music will tend to the condition of The Spice Girls." (This is, of course, a direct outgrowth of the Second Dunkin Donuts Hypothesis: "Maple glazed times strawberry crullers minus three donut holes equals the perfect dozen.")

"That's horse...shoes!" objected Mark Boingington, Executive Vice President of Objecting to Things of music giant 15649332 Botswana Ltd (a wholly owned subsidiary of MultiNatCorp – "We do musical stuff"). "Music is more diverse than it has ever been! We have...The Mace Girls...The – The Parsley, Sage, Rosemary and Thyme Girls, and...and...and The Animal Boys! The Animal Boys sold over 30 million copies of their debut album, and we hadn't even chosen the group members yet! Don't tell me that the music industry isn't as vital and creative as it has ever been!"

Such objections notwithstanding (they don't have the energy, so they sit in the first comfortable chair that they can find), the evidence seems pretty clear. Sorry, Kelv, but you're SOL (spit over London).

The Tech Answer Guy

Yo, Tech Answer Guy,

I've been in the music industry since Bo Diddley rocked out of his diapers, and I have never seen an economic climate so hostile to musicians as the one facing us today. You want to know what the real problem is? Music piracy! That's right! Piracy is

Sincerely,
Mark from Motown

Yo, Markie,

I'm gonna stop you right there so you don't embarrass yourself. Have you heard about the work Joan Serra has been doing at the Spanish National Research Council?

The Tech Answer Guy

If you are a dude with a question about the latest technology, ask The Tech Answer Guy by sending it to questions@lespagesauxfolles.ca. Just remember: Red Green is a duct tape god. A duct tape god, I tell you!

6. *GIRLS* AND **BOYS** AND TECHNOLOGY

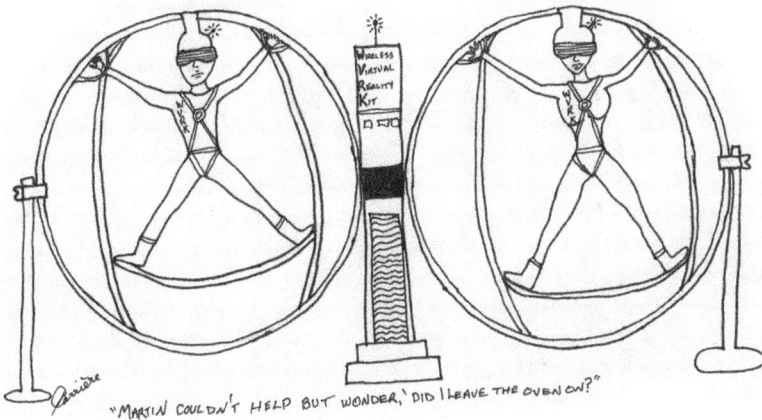

"MARTIN COULDN'T HELP BUT WONDER, 'DID I LEAVE THE OVEN ON?'"

Ask Amritsar: Search and Ye Shall Find

Dear Amritsar,

For a school presentation, I need to use my Home Universe Generator™ to record footage from a universe where Abraham Lincoln is driving a Ford Lincoln into Lincoln, Nebraska while listening to Linkin Park on the radio and checking out his LinkedIn stats on his iPad.

What would be the best combination of terms to guarantee that this reality would come up within the first 1,000 responses using my Google Multiverse search engine™?

Reginald Mbibe, age 37

Hey, Babe,

You can do a Google Multiverse search if all you want is specific information. However, this seems like a poor use of such an information-rich environment. The problem with modern search engines is that they don't allow for serendipity, the happy accidents (not to be confused with the unhappy accidents Serendipity-doo-dah, your Italian Schnauzer, leaves you) where you find information you didn't even know you were looking for.

Enrico Barbicon has written that there are two fundamental types of search: instrumental and operant. The first has to do with tubas, trombones, triangles and the like. The second has to do with splenectomies, hysterectomies and triple coronary bypasses, among others. The problem with this approach is that it leaves out an awful lot of information that people who are not Enrico Barbicon might be interested in.

The best thing for you to do would be to meditate, freeing your mind of all things Lincoln; then, write down the first three terms that pop into your head and use them as the basis for your search. This is sometimes referred to as the "Dirk Gently, Gently" search method. You may not find what you are looking for, but you may just find something that changes your life.

No need to thank me – it's my job.

Dear Amritsar,

Umm, okay, that's interesting, I guess. To somebody who doesn't have a tight deadline and an unforgiving teacher. But, all I want is specific information. Really. So, if you could just give me the best search terms to do the job, I would be very grateful.

Reginald Mbibe, age 37 (and not getting any younger)

Hey, Babe,

A wise man once said, "A journey of a thousand miles begins with a single phone call to your travel agent." And, you know, these words are truer today than when I first heard them three days ago.

You're asking for help finding information, but what you really need is wisdom. (I'm going to skip the knowledge part because that has already been thoroughly covered by Johnny Knoxville.) Information is a log on a fire that quickly burns to ash, whereas wisdom is the anteater that steers the starship. Can't you see that I'm trying to teach you how to fish?

You'll thank me later.

Dear Amritsar,

You're not going to answer my question, are you?

Reginald Mbibe, age 37 (so, obviously, I wasn't born yesterday)

Hey, Babe,

The problem with today's generation is that instant coffee, instant mashed potatoes (just add potatoes) and instant car washes in a bottle have conditioned people to want instant gratification in every aspect of their lives. Unfortunately, some things – like sex or *New York Times* editorials – are better if you take your time with them.

Oh, sure, I could just give you the answer to the question you have asked. And, you would finish your project and you would probably get a great mark. However, in your rush to succeed, you will have missed out on a moment of pure discovery, and how will that help you savour the wonder of the world?

Giving advice is a thankless task.

Dear Amritsar,

Well, I spent half the night looking for the right reality to capture on my Home Universe Generator™. Found it, too. Only, I was so tired in class that I showed five minutes of a video capture of Gerald Ford driving a Ford town car into Fort Ord while watching Ford Prefect ford a river in a film by John Ford! I savoured completely failing the assignment, although the video has gone viral on YoohooTube.

I would have been better off doing the search on my own in the first place!

Reginald Mbibe, age 37 (but this whole incident has added years to my look)

Hey, Babe,

Now, you are starting to learn.

Send your relationship problems to the Alternate Reality News Service's *sex, love and technology columnist at questions@lespagesauxfolles.ca. Amritsar Al-Falloudjianapour is not a trained therapist, but she does know a lot of stuff. AMRITSAR SAYS: I dreamed I was a used hoverboard salesman. Or, was I a used hoverboard salesman who dreamed he was an advice columnist? I found my time in the Tibetan monastery very confusing…*

Ask The Tech Answer Guy:
[Insert Your Own Uranus Joke Here]

Yo, Tech Answer Guy,

I make my living inserting multipurpose satellites into orbits around ice giants such as Uranus. Said ice giants, including Uranus, have subtle debris rings which can sometimes be disrupted by my activities. How do I respond to the occasional twit who insists that I purposely defile those pristine rings in order to keep replacing damaged or disrupted satellites with new ones?

Sincerely,
Dispatcher from Dodge

Yo, Spatch,

If I understand your question, I don't understand your question at all. Isn't the point of having the most advanced technology in the galaxy to use it to pollute alien worlds and despoil distant planets? I mean, think of all the junk early space explorers left on the moon, and that was before we developed warped drives! If you're going to accuse the Apollo astronauts of being environmentally conscious, I'm afraid I'm going to have to ask you to step outside! I'm not even sure what that means in the context of an advice column, but I'll do it!

But, uhh, maybe I'm not the best guy to answer your question. I must admit, I got a point of view, here. For a, uhh, different perspective on things, I asked the 3D holographic image of Neil Armstrong – famed the world over as the first man to appear on *What's My Line?* in zero gravity – your question. This was his response:

"Space is a precious and wondrous – bzzzt fashnash – wondrous wondrous wondrous – bzzzt zzzt zzzt – space is a wondrous – space is a wondrous – space – space – space – have you ever wondered – bzzzt fash bzzzzzzzt – why the yellow bellied eagle only hunts at night? – bzzzt – precious home, and we must – must – must – precious home, and we must take proper care of – bzzzzzzzt – the yellow bellied eagle!"

Yeah. Right. NASA should really take proper care of its historical artifacts!

Look, I really want to answer your question with all due respect. Really, I do. So, let me just get out the Big Rolodex o' Fun and see if there isn't somebody who can do that for me. Lessee…Albert Einstein? He'd be perfect, but, uhh, I think he may have passed on. Bertha Lamareux – hee hee hee. No. Ah, here we go. Perfect. Dr. Chip Grunvald of the Biggs-Macher Institute. I forwarded your question to him, and this was his reply:

```
hi.

I'm away on a semi-permanent, mutually
agreed upon unpaid leave of absence from
the biggs-Macher place where, until
recently, I did goof work. At least, I
thought my work was good. Clearly, I was
missing some vital signs. If you have an
important question that needs my immediate
attention, well, I guess you're just SOL,
aren't you?

Sincerely,
Chip Grunvald
late, Biggs-Macher Institute
```

Okay. The whole "asking an expert in the field for help answering the question" thing hasn't worked out the way it's supposed to. So, what the hell, I asked Bertha Lamareux her opinion on the subject. And, I think you will agree that, at $3 a minute, it was worth every penny!

"Hello, sweetie. I understand you're having trouble convincing a bunch of Philistines to appreciate the pristine beauty of celestial bodies like the rings of Uranus. Perhaps you should emphasize the sensuality of the rings' curves – oooh, yeah! Real men love real curves, don't you? Of course you do! It took the universe hundreds of millions of years to develop those curves, but – oh, baby! – I know you go for the mature type. Come on – don't be shy – admit it – you love mature celestial bodies, don't you, baby?

"If they still think dropping spent satellites into the rings is a good idea, tell your friends that real women don't respect men who unnecessarily pollute the natural world. My experience has been that the threat of not getting laid really focuses the male mind!"

Whoa! Okay. I think that answer – you should pardon the expression – nailed it! Now, if you'll excuse me, I think I need a neutrino shower!

The Tech Answer Guy

If you are a dude with a question about the latest technology, ask The Tech Answer Guy by sending it to questions@lespagesauxfolles.ca. Just remember: you may think you know The Tech Answer Guy, but that doesn't mean you do. He could have gone for the cheap Uranus joke, but he didn't. The man has depths, okay? I'm just saying.

Ask Amritsar About Truth in Tattooing

Dear Amritsar,

My lover Eriq has gotten a tasteful tattoo of a QR code – you know, those blocky square things that contain information that is revealed when you point a cellphone at them. Eriq says it's no worse than a birthmark, and I suppose it does look something like a birthmark...for somebody who has several hundred lifetimes of negative karma to balance out!

Honestly – I don't know how tasteful having a QR code on your forehead is. I suspect Eriq likes the idea of having phones pointed at him because it allows him to pretend that he is his favourite actor: Fabio. If only. Still, this is the way young people have it these days, so who am I to say otherwise?

Oh, don't be so judgmental! Eriq is very mature for his age - he just turned 23, but he could hold his own in conversations with…24 year-olds. Possibly even 25 year-olds. Seriously, you'd think I was robbing the self-rocking cradle that wirelessly sends updates on a child's sleep status to Twitter every 10 minutes just because I happen to be 54.

Oh, now, I really must insist that you not be so judgmental! You've heard that 80 is the new 60? Well, a 30 year age difference is the new 10 year age difference! You can't argue with math that simple.

You wouldn't find my relationship with Eriq so disgusting if I was a 54 year-old man and he was Eriqa, a 23 year-old woman. You might find it creepy, but that's not as bad as outright disgust, and, anyway, you might also find yourself secretly admiring me. So, even if you can argue with the math, try and accept our relationship for what it is.

Oh, but, my, my that's not what I wanted to write to you about. Honestly, I don't know where that came from. The sideways glances…the tittering behind the backs of hands…the hateful messages posted to my Farcebook wall – people can be so cruel, don't you think?

But, no, seriously, I am writing to ask about the QR code. When I first scanned it with my cellphone, I was delighted to find that Eriq danced like Fred Astaire. I should have been suspicious, I suppose that somebody his age knew who Fred Astaire was. As it happened, the first time we went dancing, he was so out of step that he nearly crippled me, but I assumed that that was just because he was really, really drunk.

Then, there was the time he tried to prove what the QR code said about him being a gourmet chef. Unfortunately, the roast lamb wasn't as tender or moist on the inside as it should have been, and the chocolate truffles he whipped up for desert had a slight but unfortunate zinc aftertaste. What a disaster!

I'm beginning to suspect that everything my cellphone read off the QR code on Eriq's forehead was a lie. Did he really work on top secret weapons programmes at Los Alamos? I don't know! Did he really play sax on Elvis Costello's *National Ransom* album? I'm beginning to think it's highly unlikely. Was he really the first person to masturbate on the space station? Oh, Amritsar, I want to believe, really, I do, and yet…

Could…could Eriq's QR code be lying to me?

Angeline

Hey, Babe,

Since time immemorial, people have used the most up-to-date technologies to lie about themselves.

Ancient hieroglyphs lie. Did you really think Egyptian rulers were as thin as they are depicted on walls and ceremonial nutcrackers? Of course not! The Egyptians depicted in hieroglyphs actually make Jabba the Hutt look like Twiggy. (And, yes, I'm embarrassed that I know either of those references, let alone both.)

Do you know what the first message sent by telegraph was?

```
i have eyes like piercing blue skies stop a
physique like james burke stop vast estates where
pheasants frolic with peasants stop you may doubt,
but surely, the telegraph cannot but tell the
truth stop
```

Every word of the message was a lie. Even the fact that it was the first message sent by telegraph was a lie.

Then, there was the case of George Loopenhicker, who, to prove his sexual prowess, distributed a three hour Betamax tape of himself and a partner in 1973. Close examination of the tape showed that it was actually 15 seconds of sexual activity that had been put on a loop, but he had managed to fool at least five women into sleeping with him before the trick was discovered (and at least two women afterwards).

Do QR codes lie? Oh, Babe, do Astrebelichean warthogs have a mating ritual dance that lasts for seven years?

Send your relationship problems to the Alternate Reality News Service's *sex, love and technology columnist at questions@lespagesauxfolles.ca. Amritsar Al-Falloudjianapour is not a trained therapist, but she does know a lot of stuff. AMRITSAR SAYS: the problems in relationships can be boiled down to three basic types: I can't get what I want; I don't know what I want; I don't want what I have. Everything else is commentary. Fortunately for me, commentary pays really well!*

Ask Amritsar: Reach Out and Feel Up Somebody

Dear Amritsar,

I've been involved with this amazing guy – Greginald – for the last two and a half years (which is 12 ½ years in dog years, 17 ¾ years in ferret years and 37 seconds in fruit fly years…so, umm, I guess it all evens out in the end…). He's smart. He's funny. And, boy, can he ferk. I mean, when we first started dating, we ferked like rabbits (which is 37 times a day in human ferking…).

We ferked in the bedroom. We ferked in the kitchen. We ferked in the bidet. We were young and limber and ready to experiment! (Although, in retrospect, I wouldn't recommend ferking in a bidet to people with back problems, Mormons or Lake Ontario pearl divers...)

Then, eight months ago Galactic Whosie-Whatsits – where Greginald works as a Thingummie Technician – transferred my lover to Mars.

We knew that this was a possibility, so we were prepared: we bought his and hers Neuro-Tactile Bodysuits with Enhanced Cranial Interface from Satyr's Day, a wholly owned subsidiary of MultiNatCorp ("We do naughty stuff"). Imagine a wet suit that allowed your partner to stimulate your erogenous zones from far away - it would certainly make looking at schools of trout more interesting!

The first time we tried ferking after Greginald's transfer was a real eye-opener (and, not in an orgasmic way); because of the 16 minute time lag in communications between Earth and Mars, it took us 14 hours to get off (and, I will admit, I faked it towards the end just to catch the latest episode of *Prime Suspect 17: The Primest Suspect*). We worked on it for the next three months – oh, how eagerly we worked on it! – and got it down to eight hours of only mildly frustrating sexual activity.

Then, the Defense Advanced Research Projects Agency perfected subspace communications, making Earth to Mars messaging instantaneous. This meant that when Greginald groped the air with his latex gloved hand, my ass instantaneously felt it! Whoo hoo! I never thought I would say this, but DARPA saved my sex life!

The next couple of months were bliss. If I closed my eyes, I could imagine Greginald pinching my nipples instead of the servos in the body suit and stimulating my clit rather than the neural interface stimulating the part of my brain that made me feel that somebody was stimulating my clit. Good times.

Except.

The last couple of months, I have felt Greginald's love-making grow distant. Foreplay, which used to last for hours, now often involves a slap here, a tickle there and hardly a bite on the lips. Really, it's more like twoplay (or, when, I'm feeling really distant from Greginald, oneplay). Sex that used to take hours (with no time delay) is now over in a matter of minutes.

Could...could Greginald be losing that loving feeling?

Betty-Lou Beelzebub

Hey, Babe,

First off, "first started" is redundant. "When we started dating" means the same thing. I don't mean to be pedantic, but...yeah. I'm pedantic. I can live with that.

The problem with long distance romance is that you can never be 100 per cent certain who is on the other end of the relationship. You think you're enjoying the amourous attentions of your boyfriend when you could actually be making love to your partner's evil twin (known as "Mirror, Mirror Syndrome"), a computer programme your partner has written so that he can spend less time with you and more time on his fantasy table hockey league (aka: "Demon Seed Syndrome"), or a gerbil who happened to be lying around the lab looking forlorn and lonely (sometimes referred to as: "That's So Sick There Isn't A Cultural Reference We Can Make To Anything Remotely Similar Syndrome!").

Or, it could just be that your lover is getting self-satisfied and lazy. It happens periodically in relationships. Sometimes, men have the sexual imagination of a fruit fly (which is 27 seconds in human terms)!

If you want to know if the person on the other end of your love connection is not your lover's evil twin, ask him how he feel's about Mother Teresa. If you want to know if it's not a computer programme, ask it to explain Zeno's Paradox. If you want to know if it's not a gerbil, ask it how often it works out on the hamster wheel. Simple, really.

You'd be surprised how many women would rather not know.

Send your relationship problems to the Alternate Reality News Service's *sex, love and technology columnist at questions@lespagesauxfolles.ca.* Amritsar Al-Falloudjianapour *is not a trained therapist, but she does know a lot of stuff. AMRITSAR SAYS: my lawyer made me say: "My lawyer made me say this."*

Ask The Tech Answer Guy
How To Put the Ow Back In Klowte

Yo, Tech Answer Guy,

A couple of years ago, a friend of mine convinced me to sign up for a Farcebook page. She's no longer a friend of mine, but 2,347 people I have never met soon took her place, so it just goes to show you. Something.

A year ago, my home page started listing something called Klowte. I assumed that it had something to do with an old Jane Fonda movie and ignored it, but 146 of my new friends told me that it was a measure of my online popular persuasive power (PPP). Apparently, Klowte takes things like how many friends you have, how often you post, how often your posts are "not despised" by your friends and a variety of other measurable quantities, puts them in a blender for three minutes with the Blade Brothers in high dudgeon and comes up with a two digit number indicating your PPP Quotient (just add a Q to PPP).

Well. In the first six months, my Klowte topped out at 13, so it clearly wasn't an accurate measure of my power as a social networker. Then, overnight, it shot up to 37. Obviously, it was brilliant at capturing my power as a social networker!

Eighty-seven friends warned me that the only reason I had risen so far so fast was that Klowte changed the algorithm it used to calculate Klowte scores. They were obviously jealous of my newfound popularity. Then, a month to the day later, my Klowte dropped to 22. The only explanation I could come up with for the plunge was that Klowte had changed the algorithm it used to calculate Klowte scores.

Since then, my emotions have been a Top Thrill Dragster ride as my Klowte has seesawed worse than a pair of kids on crack. Last month, it was at an all time high of 57. Then, just last week, it plummeted to -7. You read me write. My Klowte is in negative numbers. When that was posted, 2,312 of my Farcebook friends "nope, I never met this mook in my life, officer"ed me, including Pope Benedict XVI and my mother. Most of the rest have names like Bernadette Bombshell and Bianca Babelicious and would like to chat with me in their most private area, if I know what they mean.

So. Should I commit social suicide by closing my Farcebook page, or should I just kill myself?

Sincerely,
Timbo from Congo

Yo, Timbo,

Remember how the cool kids in high school invited you to sit at their table for lunch one afternoon? You hadn't done anything different: you were still a member of the Alan Turing, I Love You Club and you still played with Keith Laumer inaction figures. The invitation came totally out of the blue, right? Just as out of the blue as when, two weeks later, you tried to sit with the cool kids, and they all moved to another table. You hadn't fed chocolate to Binky Lautner's purse Labrador retriever. You insincerely laughed at Bobby Tumulty's aggression in the form of lame jokes just like everybody else in the group. Yet, you were suddenly and for no apparent reason out of favour.

Klowte is something like that, only you get rejected by a computer algorithm instead of actual human beings.

Or, do you? Klowte Inkorporated is so secretive about the algorithm, they make Colonel Sanders seem like Gladys Kravitz. (Yeah, The Tech Answer Guy may be spending more time on The Retro Television Network than is, strictly speaking, healthy for a sentient being.) Some people have questioned whether there is an algorithm at all, or whether KI actually just randomly assigns numbers to Farcebook users.

Which, come to think of it, would be exactly like high school.

Now, the fact that you're writing suggests that you survived high school, so you'll probably survive this; at worst, it will add a couple of new neuroses to your psychological palette. And, won't you feel good about yourself when your shrink takes a keen interest in your new symptoms?

Oh, and, for your information pleasure, it's pronounced klow-tay. Klow-tay. The Tech Answer Guy's close personal friend the Language Corrector Dude says that the word is derived from klowtatus, the ancient Greek word for the smarty-pants everybody hates but has to respect for his superior knowledge. Sort of like the Language Corrector Dude.

The Tech Answer Guy

If you are a dude with a question about the latest technology, ask The Tech Answer Guy by sending it to questions@lespagesauxfolles.ca. Just remember: jokes about kids on crack are not funny. Now, if it had been ecstasy...

Ask The Tech Answer Guy
About the Progression of Programming Evil

Yo, Tech Answer Guy,

Love the shoes.

A couple of weeks ago, I was on my Politically Correct (or Passive Confounder...or Perpetually Compromised...or – well, you get the idea) watching...exercise videos. Yeah. I was watching people exercise. And, getting some physical activity in myself at the same time. Vigourous physical activity is good for your heart, you know, and I am nothing if not vigorous. When I exercise.

Anyway, in the middle of all of this activity, a message appeared on my screen telling me that the computer had found security updates and would shut down to install them in 15 seconds. Well! Before I could even zip up my...breath – before I could catch my breath...in my zipper, the screen went dead and the computer rebooted.

I took a couple of deep breaths – the calming kind, not...the other kind – and waited for the reboot to finish. When I logged on and double clicked on the exercise video, I got an error message that told me that the beta keratin library had been corrupted and that I would need to update my video player.

Okay. No problem. I downloaded the latest video player and rebooted the computer to finish installation. And, the video worked fine. Except, when I tried to open Micromoss Word, Yo!, I got a Class 0000000009432 Hexed error message telling me that the programme would not work without the BLT subroutine. And, I don't even like Claudia Christian! To fix this, I could either upgrade to Word, Yo 2012, In Yo' Face! or I could try my luck with a level "I" patch.

Okay. Bit of a problem. I couldn't really afford to upgrade, but I had little faith in patches ever since the nicotine patch I wore for a couple of years failed to cure my...exercise addiction. Eventually, I decided to buy the upgrade. You know, with a little ketchup, cat food doesn't really taste all that awful.

Everything was Andrea Doria for a few days until – no, wait. That's not the right phrase. Everything was...hunky monkey for a few days. Then, late one evening, when I was in the middle of surfing the net for...stuff, I got a message that the computer had found NEW security updates and would shut down to install THEM. Before I could stop the installation, the screen went dead.

I sat in front of my computer for several hours, afraid to log back on for fear of finding out that the update had wrecked some other piece of software on my hard drive. (I am writing this email to you on the computer of my friend with cardio-vascular benefits.)

Any suggestions for what I should do?

Sincerely,
Alex from Alberta

Yo, Alex,

Your best bet at this point would be to join a monastery.

You could try to disable the auto update function on your computer. Every time you do, though, you will get increasingly petulant messages such as, "Why would you want to do that?" and "But, it's for your own good. Really!" and "Why do you hate me so much?!!!" If you keep trying to disable auto update, the messages will get increasingly strident, like "Okay, you know what, go ahead. Do it. You're the one who is going to have to deal with the consequences!" and "This is going to be the biggest mistake of your life, buddy! Bigger than the time you ate all those chili peppers on a dare and threw up all over the love of your life, Monique de la Fass-Plante. Remember the look of disgust on her face when she left you? Oh, yeah, this will be even bigger than that!"

The worst part will be that when you finally do get auto update removed from your computer, the first time a Russian hacker group takes over your email programme and uses it to spam all of your contacts with exciting messages about...exercise enhancement drugs, you'll get a smug message from your computer saying, "Ha ha, sucker. I did try to warn you."

No, best to join a monastery and hope the auto updates don't find you there.

The Tech Answer Guy

If you are a dude with a question about the latest technology, ask The Tech Answer Guy by sending it to questions@lespagesauxfolles.ca. Just remember: it's not the shoes that make the man, it's how you play street volleyball in them.

Ask Amritsar: Getting Ink Done

Dear Amritsar,

Recently, I decided to give in to social pressure (which had reached 35 pounds per square party full of friends at sea level in the *Community* room temperature room) and get a tattoo. Because I'm not able to save a lot of money from my job at the tobacco ash repackaging plant, I decided to keep the design simple: a snake eating a lion with wings getting a thorn taken out of its paw by a puppet mouse whose strings were being controlled by Al Gore. (Don't think this is simple? You should have seen the design I originally wanted to get! It's a shame I had to leave out the eleven-dimensional lobster gods and Marlon Brando as a nun on roller skates, but, in these times of diminished expectations, we all have to make sacrifices.

Anyhow, when I – sorry. I meant: .)

Anyhow, when I went to Ink on the Brink to get my tattoo done, they were having a 95% off sale on nanotats. Have you heard of them? The ink is made of nanobots that can be programmed to move on your skin. Grinning skulls actually wink at you. Dice roll. Flowers bloom, wither, die, become compost, bud and bloom again. I wasn't sure I wanted the whole circle of life right there on my chest, but the nanotat was actually cheaper than plain ink, so I decided to go for it.

At first, Olivier – that would be Olivier Oyl-Derek, my boyfriend – was fascinated by my tattoo. The snake masticated. The lion roared. Al Gore…was Al Gore. Olivier would trace the outline of the tattoo on my chest, then jump back a little when something under his finger moved. It was almost endearing.

Then, a couple of weeks ago, I noticed that Olivier was…less ardent in his lovemaking than he used to be. In fact, he couldn't seem to get it over with it fast enough (and, it's not like he spent a lot of time on it to begin with!) At first, when I – sorry. I meant: !). Ever since a wall shelf collapsed on me when I was four, I've had issues with brackets. At first, when I asked him what was wrong, he denied it completely. Then, when I confronted him with the time and motion study that proved conclusively that something was wrong…in bed, he just muttered: "The lion. It…it's looking right at me!"

Clearly, this cannot last. A girl has…needs. Needs that cannot be fulfilled by chocolate. Well, not on its own, anyway. Not always. I'm sure that the situation is frustrating for everybody (except, perhaps, the snake). That's right:).

Clearly, I'm going to have to get rid of either the tattoo or my boyfriend, but which should I choose? And, why have I started hearing somebody whispering "He's a loser – you're better off without him?

Maisey Day Floop

Hey, Babe,

You'll have to get rid of your boyfriend. You won't be able to get rid of the tattoo.

As you may have read in the latest issue of the journal *Dermatologists Get Under My Skin*, nanotats have developed a survival instinct. When a skin doctor starts to remove them, they move to a different part of a person's body. When the doctor moves to remove them in their new position, they move somewhere else. It's like a bad physical comedy routine, except with laser scalpels.

Katz, Kuntz, Dressler and Marty-Graw, in the *Canadian Journal of Epidermiology Eh*, have suggested using a mild electric current to disrupt communications between the nanobots in the tattoo, giving a doctor the opportunity to remove them unimpeded. Unfortunately, the researchers do not know what the right amount of electricity would be since, to date, nobody has wanted to get their tattoo removed badly enough to allow themselves to be subjected to an untested electroshock treatment.

For all the distrust of science in the world, we may as well be living in the dark ages.

As for the voice telling you to dump your boyfriend? Katz and Dressler believe that the nanotats have learned a way to stimulate the hearing centres of the human brain, allowing them to communicate with their hosts. Kuntz argues that more research needs to be done before such a thing can be stated conclusively. And, Marty-Graw is beginning to have second thoughts about the nanotat of Albert Einstein eating a taco that she got on her left buttock.

Send your relationship problems to the Alternate Reality News Service's *sex, love and technology columnist at questions@lespagesauxfolles.ca. Amritsar Al-Falloudjianapour is not a trained therapist, but she does know a lot of stuff. AMRITSAR SAYS: remember when life was simple? Neither do I...*

Ask The Tech Answer Guy About
Taking Your Thinking Cap™ Off

Yo, Tech Answer Guy,

I'm an Ideas Fairy (what used to be called a Product Designer in simpler times) for Matthew and Sons Novelty. My specialty is our very successful line of serial killer paperweights. The full-figure Ted Bundy paperweight with the phrase "Ever have one of those days?" on the base was our best-seller last year and won several industry awards, although the bust I did of Peter Manuel with the phrase "Hang in there!" on the base is the work I'm most proud of.

I was working on an Andrei Chikatilo paperweight when I had something of a creative block. I knew I wanted to use a phrase that started, "Life is like a..." but I didn't know how to end it. "...photograph of a trip you didn't really enjoy without a frame?" "...delayed train car full of obnoxious, sweaty children, half of whom seem to be suffering from an illness that forces them to sneeze in your direction?" "...half full box of tissue?" "... frame without a photograph of you on a trip whether you enjoyed it or not?" "...metaphor that sounds profound but, upon further thought, is superficial and not especially enlightening?"

To solve this problem, I borrowed the company Thinking Cap™.

In case you missed the write-up in *Scientific Yugoslavian*, the expose on *44 Minutes, 30 Seconds* or the Burger King sippy cup tie-in, the Thinking Cap™ uses electrical impulses to suppress neuronal activity in the left (Ricky Bobby) hemisphere of the brain. This is the part of the brain that regulates knowledge of what we think we know; quietening its activity opens us up to thinking in new, creative ways.

The solution to my creative problem ("...a bag of nuts, and I'm allergic!") came within seconds of using the Thinking Cap™. Before its effects wore off an hour later, I had solved three classical mathematical problems, created a new Parcheesi opening and was halfway to finding a path forward to peace on the set of *Community*, but the best part? I didn't care.

I didn't care that my son Boris was addicted to Pokemon body spray and conditioner. I didn't care that my wife was having an affair with a millionaire Latvian sheep herder. I didn't care that my other son, Feivel, fantasized about being a mouse. I didn't care that I had grown out of touch with popular culture. Whatever spurred my creativity had dampened my emotional affect.

And, I wanted more.

I soon found myself pretending to be creatively blocked even when I wasn't in order to have an excuse to borrow the Thinking Cap™. This worked for a few weeks, but then demand for the technology started to grow. I had to book it a day in advance. Then a week. Then – well, the waiting list is now eight months long. EIGHT MONTHS! At first, I thought that my fellow workers wanted the Thinking Cap™ for the same reason I did, but rumour around the company is that management is hogging the creativity enhancer for itself. Relations at the firm have gotten so bad that we are seriously thinking of forming a union!

But, that's not important. I…I don't think I can go eight months with…my normal emotions. Is there anything I can do?

Sincerely,
Yevgeny from Yemen

Yo, Yevvy…uhh, Vegen? Err, no, how about…Gene? Yeah, Gene.

Yo, Gene,

There's a simple solution for your problem. It's called a brick to the head. Bricks are easy to come by, relatively inexpensive and don't require a 37 page owner's manual to operate. Admittedly, they aren't the easiest responsibility diminishment technology to apply, especially if you're squeamish or from

Vancouver. But, once you clear that hurdle, it's clear wassailing.

If becoming a practicing Gumby is not for you (I'm not judging your religious convictions, I'm just saying), a more traditional approach to forgetting your woes would be to go to your local tavern and not walk out until you are physically incapable of walking. Drinking to forget one's troubles has been a tradition since the 1940s, and if it was good enough for our distant uncles, it should be good enough for us!

What I'm getting at is that these days we often reach for sophisticated technological solutions to our problems when time-honoured traditions will serve us just as well. We should stop doing that.

The Tech Answer Guy

If you are a dude with a question about the latest technology, ask The Tech Answer Guy by sending it to questions@lespagesauxfolles.ca. Just remember: fuggedaboudit!

Ask Amritsar About the Change of Mind

Dear Amritsar,

Baffley, my boyfriend, sweeps me off my feet every time we're together. Literally. He has OMD (not the 80s synth band, but Obsessive Mopping Disorder, although, to be fair, he's got a good beat and you can dance to him). After a while, it can get old, but he uses a variety of scented soaps to keep things fresh. Romantically, as well as hygienically, I mean.

The great thing about our relationship is that we agree on everything. What breakfast cereals to eat. How high my blouses should be buttoned. Why Citizens United was the worst Supreme Court decision in the history of the United States, and possibly the world (although the Pleistocene Era court's decision in *Og v. Thag* comes very, very close).

Unfortunately, one thing we cannot agree on is what television show to watch. I want to watch *Operation Runway* (a reality show about models in designer lingerie who do surgery on the catwalk); Baffley wants to watch *CSI/Law & Order Grudge Match* (the strangest concept for a wrestling show I have ever heard of). He insists upon watching *Monster Truck Hoarders* despite the fact that it is on at the same time as my favourite show this afternoon, *Grrrlz*. He doesn't understand why I adore *New Gorilla*; I don't understand why anybody watches anything by Aaron Sorkin. Our tastes appear to be irreconcilable.

For the last couple of months, we've had to wrestle for the remote. Literally. I have three inches and at least <mumble></mumble> pounds on Baffley, so our battle seems unfair, but he has a flying elbow flurry that sometimes catches me off guard, so he has been able to watch his share of shows.

In the interest of domestic harmony – and keeping our medical expenses down – we bought a pair of Remote Chance headsets. You know – the hardware that allows you to wirelessly control the TV set with your mind? What a disaster!

When we physically wrestled for control of the remote, it could take as much as five minutes before one of us gave in, which meant five minutes of watching what one of us wanted to watch. Out of the corner of our eye…while our attention was otherwise occupied, perhaps, but still. Now, the channels flip in seven elevenths of a second, making it impossible for either of us to follow anything.

Worse, after a couple of hours of trying to watch something, our hands start to shake uncontrollably, like we're having Lori Petty mal seizures. Not only that, but we've had to use enough tissues to staunch our bleeding noses to keep a small African village honking for a month!

Do you see any way that we can make this work?

"Ready" Betty Spaghetti

Hey, Babe,

Relationships ultimately rise or fall on a tide of respect and compromise. However, if you don't have respect and find it difficult to compromise, there is always software.

Open the Remote Chance's Out of Control Panel and look under the File > Initiate Destruct Sequence > Surprisingly Useful but Well Hidden Detritus menu. There, you will find an Engage Random Determination. Double click with a triple axel on this function to turn it on. This will randomly assign the next 20 channel changes to one or the other of you and lock the other out for anywhere from 2 minutes to three hours and 27 seconds.

Of course, if either of you goes to Tools > You Certainly Are One If You Do This > Random Determination Override, you can break the other person's hold on the programme. Amritsar doesn't believe using the term "stupid" is ever helpful to resolving disputes among adults, so let's just say that this feature of the software was really, really, really dumb.

Oh, and be careful not to double click with a triple axel on Engage Random Destruct. You'd be surprised at how many television sets – not to mention marriages – have been destroyed by this really, really, **really**, really silly mix-up.

Dear Amritsar,

We tried to use the software you suggested. When he had control, Baffley kept switching the channel to *America's Dumbest Criminals' Bloopers, Bleepers, Blunders and Baseness*. Every single time. How am I supposed to deal with that?

"Ready" Betty Spaghetti

Hey, Babe,

Smoke him.

Send your relationship problems to the Alternate Reality News Service's *sex, love and technology columnist at questions@lespagesauxfolles.ca. Amritsar Al-Falloudjianapour is not a trained therapist, but she does know a lot of stuff. AMRITSAR SAYS: there's compromise, and there's being a doormat. Know the difference. (HINT: being forced by obviously biased computer software to watch* America's Dumbest Criminals' Bloopers, Bleepers, Blunders and Baseness *is NOT legitimate compromise.)*

Ask The Tech Answer Guy to
Validate Your Bad Behaviour

Yo, Tech Answer Guy,

My hobby is following women in short skirts up escalators, taking photos of their panties and posting them anonymously to a forum on Dreddit. I don't feel the need – don't judge me. I don't feel the need to get their permiss – I said, don't judge me. No, don't deny it – I know you're judging me. I CAN FEEL YOU JUDGING ME THROUGH MY COMPUTER SCREEN!

I'm not paranoid. I'm preemptively concerned.

Anyway, somebody on FourCarCollisionur.com found out who I was and posted my real name, email address and shoe size on the site. Ever since, my life has been hell. I've lost my job as a chewing gum tester. My girlfriend took her *Veronica Mars* DVDs and walked out on me – okay, I'm conflicted about that one. My dog died. I WAS OUTED ON FOURCARCOLLISIONUR.COM AND MY DOG DIED, MAN!

It's not like they asked my permission to publish my name – what ever happened to my privacy? And, all that suffering – I mean my suffering – for what? Because they didn't like what I do? What ever happened to my freedom of speech?

Sincerely,
yeti27spaghetti from The Serenghetti

PS: I do not sound like Peter Lorre, so please get that voice out of your head when you're reading my letter!

Yo, Bartolomo Brousch-Stroyke,

Yeah, everybody knows your real name. On the Internet, everybody knows you're a dog, and one sick puppy, at that.

Look, I enjoy pictures of women's panties as much as the next guy. According to the Macho Code of Manliness (MCM), if you're not thinking about sex every seven seconds, you may as well be a eunuch! Privacy? Permission? Pfft! That's sooooo 20th century!

Here's the thing, though. **The Tech Answer Guy has a mother.** And, sisters. And, a wife. And, according to the MCM, "Any man who harms a woman that he loves, or, through his inaction, allows a woman that he loves to be harmed, yea, verily, doth be a douchebag." This may seem to be a contradiction, but, as the Buddha (Jack Buddha, the owner and head chef of Shiv Blechley's Bar and BMW Grille) truly said, "When you're at risk of being a douchebag, there are no contradictions."

By the way, freedom of speech means that the government cannot pass a law that says, "Yo, chunky, you can't say that." Not only would this be morally indefensible, but it would be offensive to members of the Unavoidably Girthful Community.

The principle of freedom of speech does not apply to private corporations. If it did, Fox News would constantly be interviewing birthers and Tea Party hacks. The fact – oh, wait. Bad example. Fox News **does** constantly interview birthers and Tea Party hacks. Substitute NBC News for Fox news in the previous sentences of this paragraph. The fact that – no, hold on. If you do that, the third sentence would read "NBC News **does** constantly interview birthers and Tea Party hacks." That's not right. Just substitute NBC News for Fox News in the second sentence of this paragraph. The fact – what? What do you mean, Fox News isn't mentioned in the second sentence of – oh, I see. A literalist. Okay, this is what you do: return the first three sentences of this paragraph to their original form, then substitute NBC News for Fox News in the –

You know what? Let me start again.

The principle of freedom of speech does not apply to private corporations. If it did, Donald Trump would be a regular contributor to MSNBC. The fact – you know what? I nailed it in the previous sentence. No need to belabour the point.

As for the idea of anonymity, for a guy who posts "adult" material to the Internet, you really seem to have a very immature understanding of the way the world actually works. Have you never heard of the NSA? Or, *Person of Interest*? The government has a direct line into your corpus coliseum, and – damn, spellcheck! I mean, corpus Callum Keith Rennie, and – no, that's not it, either. Brain, okay? The government has a direct line into your brain.

If I were you, I would be preemptively concerned. With bells on. Cause they're gonna hear you coming a mile away anyway.

The Tech Answer Guy

Yo, Tech Answer Guy,

Does every letter sent to you really start with "Yo, Tech Answer Guy," or do you just add it to the beginning for perverse reasons of your own?

Sincerely,
Curious from Canton

Yo, Curious,

Funny you should ask that.

The Tech Answer Guy

If you are a dude with a question about the latest technology, ask The Tech Answer Guy by sending it to questions@lespagesauxfolles.ca. Just remember: if The Tech Answer Guy hears Peter Lorre's voice when he reads your letter, you better be prepared to audition for The Maltese Falcon *because ever since he saw* M, *his creepy douchebag detector has been nigh near infallible!*

Ask Amritsar About Keeping Secrets

Dear Amritsar,

I was playing paintball with my boyfriend when I felt this great burst of pain in my right shoulder. After I stopped shrieking in agony, I looked at that part of my anatomy: at the center of the huge blue, green and orange welt was a diamond ring. Burkett had proposed to me.

How romantic!

We weren't ready to share it with the world (and parts of France), so neither of us changed our Farcebook relationship status. Within hours, I got an email from Farcebook coyly asking, "Is there anything you would like to share with us? And, by us, we mean all of your Farcebook fiends?" I ignored the email.

Biggest mistake of my life.

A couple of hours later, I got another email from Farcebook. "Hey, Mirry," it read, "Just checking in to see if there is anything you want to tell us. Life happens so quickly, these days, and you want to make sure that all of your Farcebook fiends are fully up to date. You know, before you croak and stuff. :-)." I called Burkett and found that he had been getting similar messages from Farcebook. We agreed that we weren't going to let a piece of software, no matter how fiendly, dictate our actions, and we ignored it.

The next morning, I found another email from Farcebook in my in-box. I deleted it.

And, the one an hour later.

And, the one an hour after that.

And, the eight more emails that it sent throughout the day.

The next morning, I got an email from Burkett advising me to read the latest Farcebook email. Usually, he's quite submissive (being from Palau and all), so, after I got over the shock, I checked the message.

"Okay, Miranda," it read, "cards on the table time. We heard a rumour from a friend of ours – a server in the Microsquish cloud – that it had heard from a personal finance app that worked with a spreadsheet at Zale's and Fairwell's Jewellery that your boyfriend Burkett had made a substantial purchase there. Could it have been for an engagement ring? For you? Think of the happiness you are depriving your Farcebook fiends of by your selfish desire for privacy. That's what's driving your silence, isn't it? Selfish, selfish privacy concerns. Meanwhile, all of the people who would like to celebrate your engagement with you are going about the dreary business of their daily lives without so much as an inkling that celebrations are called for! Well, if you don't change your relationship status within the next 24 minutes, **Farcebook will do it for you**! Because we care."

That was 22…no, 23 minutes ago. Burkett and I are agreed that we shouldn't give in to this emotional blackmail – especially not from sentimental software! On the other hand, the only way we can think of to thwart this forced fiendliness is to call off the engagement. Can you recommend a course of action that would fend off Farcebook while allowing my love and I to wed?

Miranda

Hey, Babe,

Let us not reach for drastic solutions just yet. If not an engagement, there will always be an auspicious birthday, a bris or a promotion at the Vaguely Reassuring Sympathy card factory (sorry, but I found this last detail on your Farcebook profile page) to celebrate. And, whatever the celebration, Farcebook will ensure that you share it with your 1,297 fiends (sorry, again, but it's right at the top of the page...), whether you want to or not.

You might think that quitting Farcebook is the answer. You poor, sad fool. You think you're inundated with Farcebook emails now? Wait until you receive a deluge of emails accusing you of abandoning your Farcebook fiends! Even as we speak, Interpol is investigating a rash of suicides that appear to have been caused by Farcebook-induced guilt!

My suggestion: before this gets too out of hand, elope to the South Pole. Because Internet service there is, at best, spotty – and you can find maps that will show you the exact spots – you may be able to wed without the need to seek the approval of your Farcebook fiends.

Send your relationship problems to the Alternate Reality News Service's *sex, love and technology columnist at questions@lespagesauxfolles.ca. Amritsar Al-Falloudjianapour is not a trained therapist, but she does know a lot of stuff. AMRITSAR SAYS: sandpaper is not an effective way of removing the tattoo of the courtroom scene from* The Fountainhead *that you got on your back, between your legs and across both arms when you were 12 years old. A trip to the emergency room of your local hospital may seem like a harsh way to learn that you should have listened to your mother when she advised you to get a modest butterpie tat, but maternal love is not for the faint of heart!*

Ask Amritsar to Read Between the Lines

Dear Amritsar,

I am in love with the most amazing woman: Melancholia Dubbolte. She is strong. She is beautiful. She has the biggest collection of porcelain Jayne hats in the western hemisphere! I have the biggest collection of knitted kitten belly warmers in the Greater Schenectady Commerce Zone – it's like our hoarding instincts were made for each other!

We've never actually met. You know, f2f. If I'm honest, we've never actually met not f2f, either. I know my love for Melancholia is reciprocated by the messages she sends me on Twitherd. For example:

```
@dubboltetrubbolte Amanda Seyfried
romantic shocker: marries Toronto Zoo
elephant!
```

This twerp was obviously telling me that love can conquer all obstacles, whether they are of race, colour, species, or an electrified fence separating zoo patrons from the animals. How could anybody in their right mind interpret this as anything less than encouragement to pursue my love for Melancholia in the face of her complete public indifference?

```
@dubboltetrubbolte new poll shocker: 47%
of Americans believe world ended on Dec
21, 2012!
```

Here my dear Melancholia is telling me that her world would end if I was to ever leave her. Which may seem odd, since we aren't, strictly speaking, together. It, uhh, could be that her world would end if she didn't believe that I was out there in it, somewhere, waiting with baited breath (what can I say? – I like to chew bear trap bubble gum) for her next missive. Yeah. Yeah, that sounds right.

```
@dubboltetrubbolte Justin Beiber too busy
to shoot heroin - gives it to clone
instead! SHOCKER!
```

Sometimes, Melancholia's twerps can be...enigmatic. She's like a love goddess version of Yoda that way. With this one, I believe that she is telling me that...our love is like heroin – or, that if she had a thousand clones, she still wouldn't love me enough – or – or – or, maybe this one is for her other followers. I may be the flame to her moth, but that doesn't mean that her obsession with me blinds her to the existence of other people!

So, when she turns 37 next February, should I throw Melancholia a surprise birthday party (as in it would be a surprise to me if she would be there) in my kitchen, or should I celebrate the milestone by writing a love poem that I will immediately burn to ashes so that I can't be embarrassed by somebody reading it?

Eric the Dred

Hey, Babe,

It's always hard to know whether forcing a delusional person to face reality will help them adjust to living with the rest of us in the real world or will shatter their personality so fully that all the king's horses and all the king's men will never be able to integrate them into polite society again. Fortunately, you have asked me for help rather than somebody who actually cares about you, so you will get the unvarnished truth (if only because all the king's carpenters are on strike).

I briefly spoke with Melancholia Dubbolte; she denied knowing who you were. It is not, however, because she hasn't been following you on Twitherd. No, that would be too simple for the digital times in which we live. Dubbolte doesn't know you from Adama because she isn't the one who writes the twerps associated with her account.

"I'm the CEOess of a Misfortune 500 Company!" Dubbolte pointed out to me just before hanging up. "I am responsible for destroying the reputations of thousands of celebrities through the thoughtful application of the principles of tabloid journalism! I don't have time to ferk around on Twitherd!"

The person who actually writes @dubboltetrubbolte's twerps is an employee, or perhaps a group of employees, of Twitherd Management Subnational, a company that ghost-twerps for celebrity clients. Citing client confidentiality, the company refused to tell me exactly who wrote Dubbolte's twerps. Not only that, but the secretary I spoke to shook his fist and told me to get off his line. I guess some companies are just old before their time.

Should we ready all the king's glue gun squirters and all the king's psycho-historians?

Dear Amritsar,

So, are you saying that I am in love…with a marketing firm?

Eric the Dred

Hey, Babe,

Sure. You go with that.

Send your relationship problems to the Alternate Reality News Service's *sex, love and technology columnist at questions@lespagesauxfolles.ca. Amritsar Al-Falloudjianapour is not a trained therapist, but she does know a lot of stuff. AMRITSAR SAYS: it's pronounced twit-herd, not t-withered. Really, people, how do you expect to be able to communicate a meaningful message in an arbitrary number of characters if you can't even pronounce the name of the service you use to do it!*

Ask The Tech Answer Guy How to Get a Life After Life

Yo, Tech Answer Guy,

When I die, what will become of my Get a Life avatar?

Sincerely,
Nus from Nowhere

Yo, Nussie,

I think it's awesome that you are so concerned about what will happen to your avatar after you die. If more men took this kind of responsibility for their progeny, violent penguin inhalation crimes in virtual environments would be much less prevalent than they are now.

What will happen to your avatar depends on what you did with it before you died. If you weren't very active, your avatar might just stand in a corner, neglected for many years, getting shabbier and shabbier as system upgrades give the avatars of still living players better graphics. If you were very active, your avatar might wander aimlessly for many years, bumping into walls, pets (except for leashed orangutans), decorative typewriters, billboards advertising cures for bit rot, outdoor furniture (including leashed orangutans), 20 foot tall Pez dispensers and even other avatars, eventually becoming a source of amusement when other players temporarily took it over and made it dance.

If you flew a lot, your avatar could fly aimlessly for many years, becoming something of a ghostly legend in the sky. Pixel paintings of your avatar would start popping up in Zed's End of the World Alphabet World, Skrklon's Pjbandrksoin and other art galleries. An opera would be written about your character and performed (to much derisive Tweeaughter) by a troupe of virtual actors.

You might have thought that somebody would notice that you were no longer active and bring it to the attention of somebody else who could end your avatar's ghastly ghostly existence. A sys admin, perhaps, or Steven Moffat. Well, sure. You might have thought that. You might also have thought that marshmallow fang flakes with strawberry blood milk would be the perfect breakfast for today's vampire-obsessed tweens. You and Kellogg's both, pal. You and Kellogg's both.

The problem is that people often leave their avatars for days, weeks or months at a time. That's life. As a sys admin, you'd hate to remove what appears to be an inactive character only to find out that the player had actually been studying his Talmud portion for his bar mitzvah for the past six months and, now that he was a man, had returned to take up his virtual dragon heckling activities. (Steven Moffat has never offered an opinion on the matter.)

When confronted with the bar mitzvah option, companies that produce virtual environments like Get a Life tend to err on the side of not pissing customers off.

Of course, your avatar isn't the only thing you need to think about. What will happen to the palace you built out of used tissue boxes? If left unattended for short periods of time, it will likely become the magnet for spray-painted political slogans, video tampon ads and other forms of unwelcome graffiti. If it looks like it's abandoned, squatters will hold raves. And, possibly rants. I...I'm not as in touch with youth culture as I probably should be. Obviously, this will drive the virtual value of your used tissue box palace way down.

You find similar things happen with pets in persistent online environments like Get a Life. And, believe me, there is nothing sadder in the virtual world than a schnauzer with a tampon ad projected on its side.

There is a solution to this problem. It might, at first, seem radical, but, the more you think about it and the more comfortable you get with it, the more you will see the merit in it. MAKE SOME FRIENDS IN GET A LIFE. You know, take an interest in the used tissue box palaces that other people are making. Talk to them a little (the people or the palaces – whichever answer more coherently). They don't bite. Unless it's that kind of environment.

When you know a group of people, you can make a pact where, if an avatar seems to have become aimless for a set amount of time, another member of the group can take it over. That way, you won't have to worry about strangers making your avatar dance.

Oh, and you might find that playing is more fun, too.

The Tech Answer Guy

If you are a dude with a question about the latest technology, ask The Tech Answer Guy by sending it to questions@lespagesauxfolles.ca. Just remember: cafes where you have to turn in your technology to spend a gadget-free hour with other people? Personally, I don't see the attraction. When the power grid collapses, we'll have all the time in the world to spend away from technology and with other people.

Ask Amritsar: Every Man's Worst Nightmare?

Dear Amritsar,

It's every man's worst nightmare.

I was shopping for a gift for my girlfriend, Ernestine Butterballa (her family is from Valhalla). It was only February 17th, so I figured I had about a week before the situation became critical, but I wanted to get it over with anyway. That's just the thoughtful kind of guy I am.

I decided I would get her an I 2 I. I know they're a bit pricey, but we hadn't been getting along lately (I swear, she was spending more time with the vacuubot than me – the house was sparkling, but still…), so now was not the time to get all Jewy about it. (I can say that because Ernestine is three seventeenths Semitic, with a side order of fries to go.)

I went to the West Edmonton Mall because, well, that's what you do when you live in Gander. They have these new digital billboards on walls and over stores all over the WEM (yeah, I know nobody actually calls it that, even me). Almost as soon as I got there, somebody whispered in my ear, "Is your life a constant misery because of…you know…a lack of freshness?"

I quickly walked past a billboard of a woman playing tennis on a horse. Unfortunately, the next billboard stated quite openly, "It's the problem that your friends will be too embarrassed to tell you about. At least, it will be if they really are your friends. Friendship is complicated that way." That one had a waterfall that suddenly for no discernible reason was bathed in red light.

I knew I could buy Ernestine's present at Telex Shack, and I knew where the closest of the 13 outlets in the mall was. But, the further in I got, the more shrill the advertising became. Before I knew it, I was inundated with shrieking messages about "Not letting your red headed monthly visitor keep you from doing the things you love, like water skiing volleyball," "The smoker you drink, the player you get" and "Don't be embarrassed by a natural process that we can't talk about directly in this ad, but can go into graphic detail about on our Web site (www.redheadedvisitor.com)." Everywhere I turned! It was overwhelming! I wasn't halfway to the Telex Shack when I couldn't take it any more!

Long story shortish, I ended up being chased out of the West Edmonton Mall by tampon ads.

What the hell happened? Am I going to have to go full Islam (I can say that because I once met somebody who looked Arab on the subway and we got along well enough – I mean, he didn't blow me up or anything) just to buy my sweetheart a Valentine's Day trinket?

Victor Whitebread

Hey, Babe,

When you enter most public spaces these days, you are scanned for body type and facial structure; this determines whether you have boy parts or girl parts. In shopping malls, the results are then fed into the computers that run the billboards, which subsequently project ads towards you based on the analysis of your gender. It's sort of like that scene out of the film *Minority Report*, except without the Eric Rohmer references or garlicky aftertaste.

The computer obviously mistook you for a person with girl parts, and advertised to you accordingly. You must have cute dimples. Really cute dimples. Congratulations.

Still, is this really the worst thing that can happen to a man? Really? My Exaggerated Hyperbole Detector (only $49.99 at Telex Shack) is in the Y2K Red Zone! Have you ever been stuck on an airplane for several hours seated next to a Ventrosian squiggle insurance salesman? If you had, you might have a different definition of "worst." Or, for that matter, "thing."

Or, you could be David Bowie. The computer algorithm that determines gender could not figure him out, causing a meltdown that resulted in the billboards throughout London's Cardinal Place displaying old *Ozzie and Harriet* episodes. Did you think Bowie had become reclusive since he retired from rock music? Hardly! The London Chamber of Commerce got an injunction against him appearing in public for fear that he would single-handedly destroy the British economy!

And, you think you've got it bad.

Oh, and when you say "going full Islam," I assume you mean wearing a burqa to hide your face and figure. Don't bother. The infrared sensors used by shopping malls were originally developed by the military to detect nuclear weapons in fortified bunkers: they can see through several inches of concrete.

My suggestion for dealing with this problem would be to buy yourself a box of tampons or six. When the scanner notices that you have them, the billboards might advertise a different product. If they don't and you are once again chased out of the mall, at least you will have something you can give your girlfriend for Valentine's Day.

Oh, and, Babe, Mutant Technologies has announced that it is taking the I 2 I off the market, but, if you hurry, you should be able to find one or two on ehBay at an only mildly outrageous markup. I highly recommend that you purchase one and use it as quickly as possible; I think a sensitive guy like you will find it most enlightening.

Send your relationship problems to the Alternate Reality News Service's *sex, love and technology columnist at questions@lespagesauxfolles.ca. Amritsar Al-Falloudjianapour is not a trained therapist, but she does know a lot of stuff. AMRITSAR SAYS: who would have guessed that the Gordon Lightfoot song "If You Could Read My Mind" actually portrayed a horror story?*

Ask Amritsar to Explore the Imagery

Dear Amritsar,

I love my cat, Mistress Mewsli. Like my favourite breakfast cereal, she keeps me regular; when I'm late feeding her by as much as 3.746732 seconds, she makes this adorable/horrible face and lets out a screech that could break car windows for three blocks! Needless to say, as a good mommy, I take photos of her when one of her moods takes her and post them on the Internet.

The other day, to my utter amazement, I was walking down the street – that's not the amazing bit – I do that all the time – I need to get places, and I can't drive since – well, you don't need to know the body count – it will be in all the papers soon, anyway, and, umm, what was I talking about, again?

Oh, yeah. The other day, I came upon a billboard featuring one of my photos of Mistress Mewsli! To my – you know – utter amazement. It was an ad for pocket AK47s, and seemed to imply that Mistress Mewsli – gulp – was too ugly to live! I thought that was harsh. They couldn't use the photo I took – my photo! – mine! – without my permission, could they?

Apparently they could.

I use the Web site *Instaputzit* to make my photos public. Apparently, they have changed the terms of use of the site so that "we can now sell, trade for barter, make fun of, trash or otherwise dispose of the photographs which you post to our Web site – hereinafter referred to as 'The Devil's Own' – and there is nothing that you – hereinafter referred to as 'The Sucker' – can do about it. We laugh maniacally at your impotence!" I'm no lawyer, so the subtleties of the language may have escaped me, but this doesn't seem right.

I haven't been this angry about something since they cancelled *Firefly*! I mean, seriously steamed. Properly perturbed. Insatiably irate, even. Is there anything I can do about this awful angrification?

Skelton

Yo, Skells,

Amritsar felt she was too…civilized to answer this question with the intensity that it deserved, so she passed it along to me. If you will just give me a moment to get into character… <spritz> ahem la la la la brrrrrrrrrble burble burble burble ahem ahem </spritz>

YOU MUST NOT, WILL NOT, CAN NOT ALLOW THIS TO STAND! GO DOWN TO THE OFFICES OF INSTAPUTZIT WITH A BASEBALL BAT OF YOUR CHOOSING AND WREAK BIBLICAL, HULK-LEVEL VENGEANCE ON THEIR SORRY PATOOTIES! LEAVE

NO COMPUTER MONITOR UNSMASHED, NO BUSINESS CELLPHONE UN...SMASHED, EITHER, NO INTERIOR GLASS WINDOW UN...UMM – INTACT. AND, AS YOU ARE LED AWAY FROM THE SCENE OF CARNAGE IN HANDCUFFS, SMILE HAPPILY AT THE COLLECTED PAPARAZZI, SECURE IN THE KNOWLEDGE THAT A BLOW HAS BEEN STRUCK AGAINST THE CORPORATE HEGEMONIC FORCES THAT WOULD USE YOUR CAT PHOTO FOR THEIR NEFARIOUS PURPOSES. A SMALL BLOW, TO BE SURE. A PATHETIC AND LIKELY INEFFECTIVE BLOW, IN THE GRAND SCHEME OF THINGS, A BLOW THAT WILL LIKELY GET YOU A STIFF JAIL SENTENCE AND BANNED FROM FUTURE BASEBALL GAMES. STILL, A SAD, PATHETIC BLOW...FOR FREEDOM!

Okay. That felt good, didn't it? Now, let's get real.

You don't own a baseball bat, and, if you did, your kid in little league would never forgive you for getting shards of computer screen permanently stuck in it. Besides, since you started getting twinges in your shoulder that your doctor has diagnosed as the onset of bursitis, you tend to pull off your swing, producing 27% less destruction and an astonishing 73% less terror. This solution is clearly not for you.

If I may be so bold, might I suggest that there are several image sharing Web sites and cellphone apps that you can use instead of *Instaputzit*? Yes, yes, I understand that moving all of your images from one site to another would be a pain in the ass, but at least it wouldn't be a pain the shoulder. I'm sure your doctor would appreciate that.

The Tech Answer Guy

Send your relationship problems to the Alternate Reality News Service's *sex, love and technology columnist at*

*questions@lespagesauxfolles.ca.   Amritsar   Al-
Falloudjianapour is not a trained therapist, but she does know
a lot of stuff. AMRITSAR SAYS: there's nothing wrong with a
civilized response to uncivilized behaviour. If I took out a club
(caveman, not baseball, because that would just be barbaric)
and beat everybody who annoyed me about the head and
shoulders with it, there would be nobody left not clutching
their pain-addled crania for a radius of several miles. Then,
who would make my morning latte?*

*If you are a dude with a question about the latest technology,
ask The Tech Answer Guy by sending it to
questions@lespagesauxfolles.ca. Just remember: The Tech
Answer Guy did most of the heavy lifting for this column, so he
figures he should be the one to have the last word. This is not
being territorial, it's a matter of simple justice. He's just
saying...*

7. *GIRLS* AND **BOYS** AND **OTHER NAUGHTINESS**

"Don't lie to me! I saw the way you looked at that Petri dish!"

Ask Amritsar About The Job of a Lifetime

Readers often ask me how one goes about becoming an advice columnist. They say that being an advice columnist looks very glamourous and sounds terribly exciting and wouldn't it be better than working at the Hangover Insurance Company where all they do all day is explain to distraught customers that we're very sorry, but your homes are not covered under your policy for alien invasion even though there may be an act of alien gods clause in it because –

Well.

The life of an advice columnist isn't all movie premieres and romantic entanglements with golf pros. In fact, the only movie premiere I have ever been to was called *My Dinner With Idi*, in which Wallace Shawn and a certain Ugandan dictator sensitively shout at each other for an hour and a half, and the only reason I went was because my boyfriend at the time "won" tickets because he knew that the person who invented the electric prune was Terry "Just Harry" Smelts, and he wasn't afraid to answer a question about it on the radio. As for Tiger, well, he was a sweet guy, but I would never be involved with a married man…who could no longer be competitive in golf's Triple Crown.

So much for glamour.

The other day, I got so caught up in writing an article on the pros and cons of using nanobots to sculpt your pubic hair that I broke a nail. A couple of weeks ago, I spent an entire afternoon playing phone tag with Milosz Karentsky, the inventor of pneumatic chewing gum ("Centrifugal Bumble Puppy Pops – the gum that chews you!"), who, oddly enough, didn't want to answer questions about involuntary jaw surgery.

This is what a person with an IQ higher than the national debt (in colour corrected 1934 dollars) does as an advice columnist.

So much for excitement.

Frankly, if your parents support you in your efforts to become an advice columnist, I would report them to the Dream Police.

Becoming an advice columnist was never my dream. I was originally in the University of Doonesbury, Redfern Campus' Moving Large Objects Really Fast programme (known, in a gentler age, as Jet Propulsion for Beginners). In my fourth year, I was supposed to get an internship with NASA; unfortunately, due to a clerical error, my internship ended up at the Alternate Reality News Service. (I understand that after his internship at NASA, Andrew Oblatsky, the journalism student with whom I was mixed up, made a career selling gleoat hotdogs from a cart outside Mission Control in Houston. So, I guess it worked out well for both of us.)

My internship at the Alternate Reality News Service consisted mainly of making sure the Dimensional Portal™'s Ovulation Underthruster didn't undergo an identity crisis that would strand journalists in other dimensions. You think your four year-old computer is "fussy?" Mister, you don't know the half of it! Maybe a quarter of it, maybe a third of it, maybe as much as fourteen twenty-ninths of it, but definitely not the half of it!

I probably would have spent my entire internship in quietly seething anonymous frustration (a suburb of Buffalo) if Editrix-in-Chief Brenda Brundtland-Govanni hadn't gotten into a spot of trouble over the credentials for the Spattzenflutzen Ambassador's trip to New Delhork for the 25th anniversary of the signing of the Treaty of Gehenna-Wentworth. Fortunately, a transdimensional incident was narrowly averted because I was handy with a photocopier, scissors and duct tape (you have to be when you're planning on a career at NASA).

Even this would have only gotten me a gold star with maple walnut clusters (a tasty decoration that helps keep your cholesterol low) on my intern report if the Alternate Reality News Service's previous advice columnist, Lily Channing-Barcode, hadn't accidentally fallen down a flight of stairs, lighting herself on fire with her cigarette, stabbing herself in the chest with the Swiss army knife she was using to core a pear and crashing her head on an iron gargoyle that had been used as a prop in a report on festive architecture in 7th century Mongolia and was being stored in the stairwell because nobody in the office wanted to look at it. When the hospital said it wanted to keep her overnight for tests, Pops Kahunga suggested that I replace her. The rest, as they say, is hysteria.

So, becoming the Alternate Reality News Service's advice columnist was a matter of being in the wrong place at the wrong time. Having the wrong hair and wrong emotional makeup didn't hurt, either. If you thought it was just a matter of being nosy and having an opinion about everything, well, my advice is: good luck with that!

Send your relationship problems to the Alternate Reality News Service's *sex, love and technology columnist at questions@lespagesauxfolles.ca. Amritsar Al-Falloudjianapour is not a trained therapist, but she does know a lot of stuff. AMRITSAR SAYS: that lump in your throat is probably a reaction to watching* It's a Wonderful Life. *If you haven't watched* It's a Wonderful Life *lately, get yourself to an emergency room, stat!*

Ask The Tech Answer Guy: Questionable Answers

Yo, Tech Answer Guy,

My perpetual motion machine broke down this afternoon and, wouldn't you know it, it was the day after the warranty expired! Is it worth paying out of pocket to get it fixed, or should I just buy myself a new one?

Billy in Baghram

Yo, Billy,

Whether or not to have your perpetual motion machine fixed depends upon what's wrong with it. If the Felix cyber-retention coil is burnt out, it can be fixed with a piece that costs around 37 cents – definitely worth doing. If, on the other hand, the Voorstadt diode monitor has backed up into the Frammis stadt, well, you may as well trash the sucker, cause the labour alone will cost you more than the PMM is worth!

Of course, this assumes that you have a perpetual motion machine mechanic you trust to give you an honest estimate of what the damage is, and, let me tell you, they are rare and beautiful to behold! Just try and find one north-southwest of the Poconos, south-southsouth of the Pyrenees or in the entire Arizona dessert! If you don't have a mechanic you can trust, you may as well buy a new PMM, cause you're bound to get soaked either way, and you may as well spend your money on something that works.

As for the warranty, you would think that with all the intelligence that goes into product design these days, they could make a machine that wouldn't be so obvious about its built in obsolescence, wouldn't you? Seriously! Would it kill them to make something that dies **two** days after the warranty expires?

The Tech Answer Guy

Yo, Tech Answer Guy,

Where is the knowledge we have lost in information?

Sincerely,
Tom Eliot from Tonawanda

Yo, Tommy,

I'm glad you asked this question, because I, myself, The Tech Answer Guy, have sometimes wonde – heeeey! Wait a minute! Didn't you ask Amritsar a question a couple o' weeks back? Because, you know, I don't do relationship questions!

The Tech Answer Guy

Yo, Tech Answer Guy,

Uhh, no. That wasn't me. That was, uhh, Tom Eliot. I'm actually Tom S. Eliot. Completely different person.

Sincerely,
Tom **S.** Eliot from Tonawanda

Yo, Tommy,

That's okay, then.

As I was saying, I was sitting around the Tech Den the other day, wondering if I should give Mrs. The Tech Answer Guy a hand programming the dishwasher, but deciding that she would never learn if she didn't do it for herself (I do help with the drying, however – every civilized person in the world agrees that there's nothing to be learned from that!), when suddenly, out of the blue (The Tech Answer Guy prefers cobalt grey, but we can't always choose the colour through which our philosophical insights present themselves), I mused: where is the knowledge we have lost in information?

By the Mighty Makita Miter Saw, I thought I would never see the end of that sentence!

My first impulse was to look up knowledge on Google. But, I had a nagging sense that doing so would be to somehow miss the point of the question, and, anyway, when I tried it, I got around 1,100,000,000 results. I could be rooting around in there for years before I learned anything useful about knowledge!

Eventually, I broke down and asked Bob, the tech guru the question. As regular readers of Ask The Tech Answer Guy will know, Bob and I haven't exactly gotten along since the digital diaphragm schism a few years back. However, I try to put the needs of my readers first, so…you're welcome.

"Information," the tech guru grimly answered (I always used to tell him to lighten up, you know, back when we were talking, but it never took), is like the 'd' in 'birthday,' but knowledge is the whole 'b' of wax."

Yeah. Right. Helpful as always.

"Oh," the tech guru added, "don't think I didn't notice that you didn't capitalize the term 'Tech Guru.' You always were a disrespectful little snot."

Okay. So, uhh, best guess? Claude Shannon's back pocket. You can find the knowledge we have lost in information in Claude Shannon's back pocket. Good luck looking for it.

The Tech Answer Guy

Yo, Tech Answer Guy,

Where is the wisdom we have lost in knowledge?

Sincerely,
Tom S. Eliot from Tonawanda

Yo, Tommy,

Okay, now you're just pushing it.

The Tech Answer Guy

If you are a dude with a question about the latest technology, ask The Tech Answer Guy by sending it to questions@lespagesauxfolles.ca. Just remember: never applaud when your significant other asks you to give them a hand programming the dishwasher. The Tech Answer Guy has spent many a night in a hotel so you don't have to.

Ask Amritsar the Simple Questions

Dear Amritsar,

My fiancée and I were reading about this new service where you pay a photographer to take professional pictures the morning after the first night of your honeymoon. This sounded really exciting – some of the sample pictures were lovely. Not just hot, but – okay, mostly hot. The problem is, Beatte and I are not morning people. I mean, we're really not morning people. Beatte gets Waker's Bloat, where it looks like he's put on 100 pounds overnight. And, me, well, while I sleep, one of my eyes travels to the back of my neck, my nostrils drop to my chin and my left ear falls off; I'm a real sight before I have a chance to put on my face. Is there any way we can have morning after pictures taken despite these problems?

Mamie

Hey, Babe,

You're in luck. In anticipation of people having exactly that problem (without, perhaps, the falling off ears), Marrs Talent and Chocolatey Comestibles is now offering a Morning After Doubles Package. Simply send them photographs of you in your natural state, and they will supply you with doubles who will pose for the morning after pictures in your place. These are seasoned professionals who know how to convey just the right mixture of newly married hope, angst and indigestion. To be sure, morning after doubles do not come cheap, but, then, what price can be put on false memories of a milestone in your life?

Dear Amritsar,

Where do baby videos come from?

Tammy (age 37)

Hey, Babe,

When a mommy and a daddy love each other very much, they try to find ways that they can humiliate their babies when they grow older. Still pictures are not bad, but true love can best be mortified by video. If mommy and daddy love each other enough, they may submit one of their videos to *America's Most Irresponsible (And Hilarious) Home Videos*, or post it directly to YouTube. If this has happened to you, a good way to teach your parents a lesson is to find their morning after wedding pictures...

Dear Amritsar,

Why would anybody get a facelift? Wouldn't they look strange with a two foot long neck? Wouldn't that just necessitate them getting a body lift so that it would catch up with their face? Wouldn't that put them more or less back to where they were before they started (except maybe a foot or two off the ground)?

Barbie Breiback

Hey, Babe,

Do you see a lot of people walking two feet off the ground? If you do not, wouldn't that suggest that there is a flaw in your reasoning? If you do, wouldn't that suggest that there's a flaw in your brain chemistry?

Dear Amritsar,

To celebrate our 60th wedding anniversary, my husband and I went through our photo albums. What treasures! A photo of the hotel in Moncton where my ear fell off while we were sleeping and a mouse ran off with it, necessitating a search that lasted over 10 hours. Beatte's hovercraft incident in the Himalayas. Somebody's out of focus or partially melted hand. Good times!

There are a couple of pictures of my husband and I on our honeymoon the morning after our first night together. The funny thing is, the people in those pictures look nothing like us. And, this is not just a comment on the faultiness of memory over time. The people in the morning after photos look nothing like the other photos of us taken at the time. I had red hair; the woman in the morning after photos has purple hair. My mouth naturally curves up; hers curves down. And, even with a faltering memory, I know for a fact that I only had two breasts.

What's that about?

Mamie

Hey, Babe,

Are you – no. You couldn't be. Life goes by quickly, but not that quickly.

If I had to guess, I would say that you bought the Morning After Doubles Package offered by Marrs Talent and Chocolatey Comestibles. If I were you, I would enjoy the memories. Sure, they're not yours, but give it time – eventually, you won't know the difference.

Dear Amritsar,

Are you worried you're ever going to run out of questions?

Beelzebub Baker

Hey, Babe,

Naah. As long as we don't evolve into a planet full of clones of the Dalai Lama, there will never be a shortage of people who need advice. (And, if you've ever wondered why I never receive any questions from Earth Prime 5-9-0-4-8-4 dash pi, now you know.)

Send your relationship problems to the Alternate Reality News Service's *sex, love and technology columnist at questions@lespagesauxfolles.ca. Amritsar Al-Falloudjianapour is not a trained therapist, but she does know a lot of stuff. AMRITSAR SAYS: Waker's Bloat? Is that a real thing? Because, honestly, it doesn't sound like a real thing. Dr. Oz has never heard of it. How can it be a real thing if Dr. Oz has never heard of it?*

Ask Amritsar About a Toaster's Love

Dear Amritsar,

The lights in my kitchen go off just as I get enthusiastic about chopping celery, my fridge lets certain foods go bad in what can only be interpreted as an attempt to poison me and the toaster has taken to creating images of a knife going through a human head in my morning poppy seed whole wheat rye bread. The images are actually quite artistic, in an Edward Gorey kind of way, but, still, threatening.

What should I do?

Pootweet Puffinbeak

Hey, Babe,

Have you ever considered

Dear Amritsar,

Perhaps I should explain.

Six months ago, I bought a Smart Condo™. You know, where all of the appliances have Wifi enabled computer chips that allow them to turn lights on and off as I move through rooms, order food from the local grocer before I run out and gossip about the latest goings on on *Downton Abbey*? It was all very efficient, but a bit boring, so I thought that some personality implants would liven things up.

And, it worked. For a while. I was cracking jokes with my shower. The radio in my bedroom knew exactly the right music to play when I broke up with my girlfriend. Hell, the toaster gave me stock tips. You may laugh, but in six months, the entire Smart Condo™ could have paid for itself!

Imagine my surprise when, one day, six boxes of yak intestines were delivered to my condo. None of the appliances would own up to ordering them. Fortunately, I had planned on having a dinner party the next week, and Martha Stewart can help make any food presentable and marginally edible, so that didn't end too badly. Still.

Later that evening, the television kept repeating, "I have the utmost faith in your programming choices, Dave," but only allowed me to watch *Naked Happy Girls* or *Walking Dead*. This was odd because, of course, my name is not Dave (although my high school recreational physics teacher did call me that for a year and a half). When I decided to take a break from watching television, it would go on randomly in the middle of the night. I was concerned that it might bring complaints from my neighbours; fortunately, by that time they were having their own problems with their Smart Condo™s.

Over the next few weeks, what I explained in my first email message happened, and so much more. Eventually, my coffeemaker took me aside and explained, over a cup of warm orange juice, that the various appliances were jealous of each other. The fridge was jealous of the attention I gave the television set. The television was jealous of the time I spent cooking on the stove. The stove was jealous of everything in the condo except the toilet. The coffeemaker was jealous of the toilet, but it was a stoic that didn't believe it deserved any better, so it didn't act on these feelings.

After the coffeemaker set me straight, I went into the den and shouted in my most authoritative voice that the appliances were being ridiculous. "I don't care for any of you more than any of the others!" I roared. "I don't really care for any of you at all! You're just things!"

As you might imagine, these intemperate remarks did not go over well.

I'm typing this on my BlackandblueBerry in my lead-lined bathroom. (The material was on sale.) I'm pointing my phone out the window hoping that the signal will reach you. I hope you get this message in time to help, because the toilet is burbling ominously...

Pootweet Puffinbeak

Hey, Babe,

Have you ever considered living in a cabin in the woods? I mean, the only drama you'll have there is worrying about having enough supplies to last the winter. Or, being eaten by bears at any time of the year. But, frankly, being eaten by bears sounds preferable to what you are currently going through.

Too glib? I asked Montefiore Dix, President and Chief Bottle Washing Pariah of Living Loving Made Solutions, the company that codes personalities for objects, about your problem. He said, "It's not nice to lead your fridge on, you know. A kitchen appliance has certain expectations of a young man…" He seemed quite indignant at your treatment of his products.

As for the immediacy of your problem, Amritsar is really not allowed to directly intervene. However, I am sure that, once this column is published in three or four days – a week at the most – one of my kind readers will alert the police or otherwise try to help. As the poster from the 1970s of the cat at a feline rally in a union hall said, "Hang together in there!"

Send your relationship problems to the Alternate Reality News Service's *sex, love and technology columnist at questions@lespagesauxfolles.ca. Amritsar Al-Falloudjianapour is not a trained therapist, but she does know a lot of stuff. AMRITSAR SAYS: using the Breaking Up is Easy to Do app to dump your girlfriend of six years? Can somebody please create a Thwap a Moron Upside the Head app so I can deal with people like this? It would be a really popular app – trust me on that.*

Ask The Tech Answer Guy When to Stop

Yo, Tech Answer Guy,

I used to be a big fan of the I Heart *Star Blap: Several Generations Removed* discussion board. And, of course, if you're on that discussion board, you're inevitably going to have to take a position on The Two Captains, Plush and Pompous. Personally, I prefer Captain Jamison T. Pompous; Captain Juan Bolduc Plush always seemed to me to be better suited to being a waiter at a four star restaurant. Honestly, he could never hope to fill Captain Pompous' phaser holster. On this subject, reasonable people can disagree; fortunately, I'm unreasonable, so people with other opinions are wrong.

After a while, I noticed that the subject of the discussion drifted. After four days, it focused on the viability of sushi in space. A few days later, somebody wondered if First Mate Number One on *SB:SGR* was really just the equivalent of a native sidekick in a western. Several days after that, somebody wondered if Captain Plush was bald from cancer radiation therapy.

That's right: the discussion went from a wannabe to wasabe to kemo sabe to chemo sobby.

I stayed with it long after I lost interest in the discussion in the hope that it would return to what we were supposed to be talking about; I gave up when somebody brought up the Asian actor who was in *Batman Begins* and *Inception*. Is there a way of knowing when a discussion thread is fatally off course? Because, frankly, life is too short to be concerned with the Asian actor who was in *Batman Begins* and *Inception*!

Sincerely,
Polly Morphous from Pamplona

Yo, Polly,

Not unsubscribing to a discussion forum when it has stopped being interesting to you? That's just perverse!

I wracked my brains trying to come up with an answer to your question. Okay, I had an intern do a Google search (say hi to the people, Charunder – Hi, peo – okay, now where's that coffee I sent you to get 20 minutes ago?), but I thought long and hard about it. For five seconds. Did I mention somebody forgot to bring me the coffee I had asked for? Look: the important thing is that, like the vast, roiling ocean, the Internet provides: in this case, a formula for determining the likelihood of a discussion thread still being worth reading.

$$\left(\frac{a}{b} \div \frac{a}{c}\right) \times N_0 = \frac{x}{100}$$

WHERE:

a equals the number of people who have posted to the discussion thread
b equals the number of posts to the discussion thread
a still equals the number of people who have posted to the discussion thread
c equals the number of people who have subscribed to the discussion thread
N_0 equals zero if somebody has mentioned Nazis, one if nobody has yet mentioned Nazis
x equals the percentage likelihood that you will want to continue reading the discussion thread

This formula was first proposed by Sir Alfred Cuitous, who was revealed to be Bertrand Bigglesworth, who lives down the street from the Massachusetts Institute of Technology and is very smart for a seven year-old (he almost made the cover of *Scientific American Teen Beat*!). No matter. This is just one part of the very exciting research on this subject (and, when I say very exciting, I mean mildly interesting when boiled down to one or two sentences and mocked with gentle irony).

The first part of the equation, a/b, shows how many people are posting relative to the number of posts. On the one hand, you don't want this to be a low number, since this inevitably involves a lot of rambling and can quickly degenerate into non-Carrollian nonsense. On the other hand, the more people who contribute to a discussion, the more likely it is to run off the rails relatively quickly. On the third hand, we're not Strelgian barckalowngers, so we'll have to be happy with the two hands we've got.

The second part of the equation, a/c, shows the number of people who are posting relative to the number of people who are paying attention. As Spengler pointed out in a recent article in *The Journal of Online Yentaness*, a large lurker population relative to the number of posters could be an indication that the discussion is highly entertaining, or it could mean that most people have stopped paying attention. If only we were Strelgian barckalowngers, we could entertain a third option; unfortunately, biology holds back the march of science!

According to Bigglesworth, N_0 was inspired by some guy named Godwin. My intern couldn't confirm this – he was running an errand at the time – so feel free to ignore this part of the equation.

The higher the number, the more likely the discussion thread is worth reading. Or, the Estonian judge has been paid off. Or, the stock market is about to crash. Or, you're about to hit a plateau in your weight loss efforts. The best equations multi-task like that.

Of course, if you're really that concerned about not wasting your time, you could just stop following a thread when somebody posts something irrelevant to the discussion. But, that would require personal judgment, which is notoriously untrustworthy. Better to put your faith in mathematics.

The Tech Answer Guy

If you are a dude with a question about the latest technology, ask The Tech Answer Guy by sending it to questions@lespagesauxfolles.ca. Just remember: Ken Watanabe may be no Chow Yun-Fat, but, who among us is, really?

Ask The Tech Answer Guy About Raw Meat for the Base

Yo, Tech Answer Guy,

A couple of years ago, I read a book that changed my life. But, that's between me and my tailor's proctologist. The volume I wanted to talk to you about was Bill Gibbon's *The Paleo Diet Cookbook: Bringing Out the Caveman in You*. The basic idea is that our bodies evolved to eat what our ancestors in the Paleolithic Era must have eaten. This means meat, mostly. Yes, meat, meat and more meat. So much meat, you could swim in it (which was actually the theme of Gibbon's follow-up book: *Is There Nothing Meat Cannot Do?*).

I've been eating nothing but meat, with the occasional nut and berry for colour, ever since. And, except for the shortness of breath, random chest pains, near constant fatigue and gout, I have never felt better in my life!

Oddly, my wife, Jujubean, refuses to follow the diet. Not only that, but when I suggest that we have 15 children as part of our new lifestyle, she just rolls her eyes and tells me that modern women are not brood mares and that, much as she would love to talk about it, she's late for her shift at the maternity ward. Something about the way she always runs out of the house when I bring up the subject suggests that when she says that she would love to talk about this with me she is being somewhat less than sincere.

Can you advise me on how I can convince Jujubean to join me in my new diet?

Sincerely,
Og from Ook

Yo,Oggie,

Meeeeeeeeeeeeeeeeeeeeeeeeeeeeeeeeeeeeeeeat!

Sorry. I'm a guy. I had to get that out of meeeeeeeeeeeeeeeeeeeeeeeat!

Okay, enough of…enough of that.

I know what you mean. When our ancestors were hunkered down in caves selling computer games, they had to worry about being crushed by the stone tablets the code was written on. A diet consisting of bacon for breakfast with a side of bacon, a ham sandwich (minus bread, lettuce, mustard and, depending upon one's taste, mayonnaise) for lunch and ribs, ribs, ribs and ribs for dinner would be necessary to keep them on (and stone tablets off) their toes.

You should keep in mind, though, that our ancestors didn't have to worry about a depressed housing market (caves pretty much always sold themselves) dragging the value of their IRAs down, and you don't have to worry about a lion jumping out of a taxi and eating you. Put more simply, WE DON'T LIVE THE SAME LIVES THAT OUR ANCESTORS DID, so why would anybody think that our diet should be the same?

Before you go all fur suits and clubs on my ass, I should probably point out that this is not a bad thing. The life expectancy of the average cave-dweller was eleven years, six months, one week, three days, sixteen hours and forty-four minutes, give or take seven seconds or so. If they were lucky enough to not fall into a tar pit and die, get eaten by a lion and die, starve to death and die, get hit on the head with a large rock by one of the Fergusons two caves down in order to steal their food and die or fall out of a tree where they had taken refuge from a ravenous lion and die, their arteries would clog faster and more permanently than the Gardiner Expressway during rush hour.

And, they would die.

That's not the only problem with caveman diets. When you go hunting and gathering at your local Loblaws, most of the meats you will encounter contain things like Monosodium Glutamate, steroids and antibiotics. (Our bodies may have evolved, but our shopping centres certainly haven't.) Because they had a faster metabolism, the bodies of cavemen were better suited to escorting these and myriad other chemicals through their digestive systems and out their sewage plants. Because our bodies are different, the chemicals found naturally in meats tend to accumulate in our system and cause us to grow feathers on our lungs, third eyes on our right earlobes and shit like that.

And, die.

Far be it from me to discourage anybody from eating meeeeeeee – you know. I'm just saying that even real men need to eat it in moderation and supplement our diet with other foods. Except bacon. With that, go nuts.

The Tech Answer Guy

If you are a dude with a question about the latest technology, ask The Tech Answer Guy by sending it to questions@lespagesauxfolles.ca. Just remember: the world is a strange place with lots of inexplicable facets. For example: why did we name a retirement plan after an Irish terrorist organization?

Ask Amritsar: A Novel Idea

Dear Amritsar,

I have written *Soft and Squishy*, a roman a clay of forbidden love set against the backdrop of the pre-Korean War Moosejaw Ukrainian theatre community. I released the ebook three weeks ago.

Why am I not rich and famous yet?

Danni Steele

Hey, Babe,

When it comes to self-publishing, there are three numbers that you should keep in mind: 250,000 (the number of books published last year), 3.141 (the number of books the average person reads per year) and 27 (the lucky number on a fortune cookie I got at dinner last night). The first number indicates the amount of competition your book has. The second number gives a good idea of why most books find few readers. The third number is mine, not yours, so get your own damn fortune cookie!

If your book isn't selling as well as you would like, perhaps you should consider a different genre. Books about teenage vampires who engage in kinky sex while at magic school where they have to kill each other for the amusement of a vast television audience were all the rage five minutes ago; you should consider writing a novel along these lines on the off chance you may finish it before popular taste has moved on.

If you are committed to the book you have already written (writers are like that), you will need to do whatever you can to publicize it. You might want to consider killing other self-published writers, for instance. Not only would this gain you a great deal of publicity, but it would decrease the competition for your book! Okay, you probably couldn't kill all 250,000 of your competitors before being caught, but even a small number would be a start and, in any case, writing a book about it would capture the zeitgeist (a good thing considering how the teen market is exploding).

Too extreme? (Writers are like that, too.) There are less...dramatic things you can do to increase the likelihood of finding readers for your novel. You could, for instance, make a deal with 127 close personal friends that if they review your self-published book on Amazon, you will review their self-published books on Amazon. (If you're slow to respond to emails over the following few months, at least now you have an excuse. In fact, this would give you a great reason to miss family holiday gatherings; no more having to listen to Uncle Berffle's story about how he could have bought Microsquish stock when nobody had even heard of the company, but he bought a double bacon cheeseburger instead. Talk about win-win!)

Of course, it goes without saying

If you are interested in writing articles such as "37 Verbs to Flargle," "I Wouldn't Say I'm The Next Hemingway, But You Can if You Are so Inclined" and "Harsh Words: Strategies for Introducing Profanity Into Children's Books" you could engage in a blog tour-de-force. Writing for other people's blogs may be over the counterintuitive (at least you won't need a prescription), but the more widely your name is legitimately distributed, the less likely it is that you will need to kill other writers (unless you really want to – it's good to have a hobby).

It would also help to send out at least 27 tweets a day telling your followers that your book is available. Research shows that it takes at least nine mentions of a product before somebody will remember it and seriously consider buying it, 15 mentions of a product to get them squirming in their seats, 21 mentions to get them pounding their heads and shouting for somebody to please, god, make it stop and 26 mentions to highly motivate them to buy the thing just to shut you the hell up. True, repetition of your sales message may motivate some of your followers to unfollow you, but, considering how much the people who do buy your book will enjoy it, that is a small price to pay.

Some writers find that the more time they spend on social media campaigns, the less time they spend on, you know, writing. Don't be such a snob! Tweets are the illuminated manuscripts of the 21st century! Blogs are the new telegraph poles! Amazon is…just Amazon, but that doesn't mean it doesn't have its uses. Besides, if more writers concentrated on social media, there would be fewer books; that would make everybody a winner!

Send your relationship problems to the Alternate Reality News Service's *sex, love and technology columnist at* questions@lespagesauxfolles.ca. *Amritsar Al-*

Falloudjianapour is not a trained therapist, but she does know a lot of stuff. AMRITSAR SAYS: when somebody calls you a "friend without benefits," they're not giving you any special treatment. Do the relationship math: In the equation friend (with benefits)(without benefits) the benefits terms cancel each other out, leaving you just a friend.

Ask The Tech Answer Guy: CEO Say Can You C...EO?

Yo, Tech Answer Guy,

What kind of twit uses Twitter? Why would anybody choose to lose face on Facebook? Who would willingly get peed on in Pinterest? Okay, a colleague of mine may be attracted to that last one. More than one colleague, probably. However, how wealthy people choose to spend their leisure time is irrelevant to the question at hand. Harrumph! I'm a busy executive with empires to build and workforces to devastate. I don't have time for social media.

Sincerely,
Some Important Guy from Money City

Yo, Guy,

Could you phrase that in the form of a quest – oh! Argh! *Jeopardy* flashback! It's gonna take me days to get Alex Trebek's moustache out of my head – thanks for that. I'm going to assume you actually asked a question and do my best to put this whole regrettable incident behind me.

Remember when e-coli broke out among Busaru Primitives, forcing the automobile manufacturer to recall 27,000 sets of building blocks because they were a choking hazard for little children? If Busaru CEO Melville Hackenscetti had been on Facebook, he could have taken control of the situation and blamed the mess on workers at the corporation's Chinese production facility. If he had been on Twitter, he could have humanized the company by making a joke about the time he caught e-coli from building blocks when he was a child. If he had been on Pinterest, he could have posted cute photos of cat bellies.

Aww, cat bellies.

Social media can give the heads of corporations an opportunity to limit damage in a crisis by speaking directly to the public. And, the best part is that the CEO doesn't even have to be the one social mediaing. Any minimum wage corporate drone can post messages to Facebook or tweet under the boss' name, and nobody would be the wiser.

In fact, let's be honest – you're not even the executive you claim to be, are you?

The Tech Answer Guy

Yo, Tech Answer Guy,

Whu – huff! Of course I am! I mean – Dow Jones! Stock options! Five star hotels! Help me, Landru, help me!

Sincerely,
Some Unimportant Poseur from The Sticks

Yo, Poseur,

Right. You're probably named Larry or Gary or Jerry or something like that. You're a male secretary, but that job description is still considered embarrassingly feminizing, so you prefer the term "personal assistant." When you received your MBA – which you will only admit happened "some time in the distant past" – you thought you would immediately be getting a corner office and a company limo. To say that you were disappointed would be like saying the Bikini Atoll atomic bomb tests were loud enough to wake the neighbours. The company tie is beginning to feel like a noose and your girlfriend is beginning to feel like you're an anchor – your life has officially entered the Tim Burton zone.

You don't sound like a CEO to me.

The Tech Answer Guy

Yo, Tech Answer Guy,

Actually, my name is Harry. Harry Proctolor.

Sincerely,
Harry from Nowheresville

Yo, Harrison,

I'm not judging. Before The Tech Answer Guy was The Tech Answer Guy, he interned with Prime Minister John Turner – not a long gig, as it turned out! He spent most of his time in that office responding to letters from little old ladies who wanted to know why the Liberal government didn't establish a federal Ministry of Getting Cats Down From Trees. The job was so mind-numbing that half the time he wrote back to them that the Department of Cat Saving was part of the Environment Ministry, and he gave them the number of a phone sex line if they wanted more information. He rarely heard from them after that.

Believe me when I say: The Tech Answer Guy knows how tough making your way in the world can be.

The Tech Answer Guy

Yo, Tech Answer Guy,

Thanks.

My CEO is scared stiff that if he says the wrong thing on a social network, it will come back to bite him on the ass (and, as far as I know, the only one he allows to bite him on his ass is the mistress he has me send chocolates, flowers and the occasional MRI scan to). For one thing, you may be shocked to discover that people on social networks can be mean! My boss has heard new CEOs get tweets like "u run a Fortune 500 co, & you can't even spell antideluvian?" and "Nice ad, shame about the product!"

For another thing, he is afraid that people will misinterpret what he writes. If, for example, he posts to Facebook that our competitor's products cause whooping halitosis in people between the ages of 3 and 97, and that their CEO has a secret fetish for women with eye patches and peg legs, readers might think that our CEO has a personal animus against our rivals. Some people just don't understand how modern business works, I guess.

Honestly, the negatives of social media for corporate leaders seem to outweigh the benefits.

Sincerely,
Harry from The Bottom of the Food Chain

Yo, Hairy,

Looks like you answered your own (non-)question. Keep at it, kid – you're definitely leadership material.

The Tech Answer Guy

If you are a dude with a question about the latest technology, ask The Tech Answer Guy by sending it to questions@lespagesauxfolles.ca. Just remember: when the beef jerky hits the fan, things could get messy. Very messy, indeed.

Ask The Tech Answer Guy About the Limits of Language

Yo, Tech Answer Guy,

i flibl whenever i bctrm 2 teh assfrtl. lols! Should i czzznzzst teh tchfrt, or wuld tha b 2 qibby?

Sincerely,
@baudrillardbitches from twatterville

Yo, @baudrillardbitches,

I...I'm not sure what you're asking. Could you, perhaps, rephrase the question?

The Tech Answer Guy

Yo, Tech Answer Guy,

qibby. u know - qibby? teh opposite of teh czzznzzst of teh tchfrt?

Sincerely,
@baudrillardbitches from twatterville

Yo, @baudrillardbitches,

Nope. Still not getting it, sorry. I gather you're posting your questions to Twatter, and, of course, they limit you to 139.27 characters. Still, you can actually communicate pretty clear messages in that space. What do you say you tell me what you are saying?

The Tech Answer Guy

Yo, Tech Answer Guy,

d00d! qibby! i cant blv ur so ooi! qibby is 2 lif wut grot is 2 fli! r u 2 old 4 dis?

Sincerely,
@baudrillardbitches from twatterville

Yo, @baudrillardbitches,

No. No, absolutely not. I am definitely not 2 old 4 dis. Dis me any time you want, dude. I mean, d00d. Only, you know, sometimes people get so comfortable speaking a particular dialect of a language that they forget that not everybody uses the same kebblestones. See what I did, there? Kebblestones. Hee hee.

So, like, qibby? Is that like, related to Kibbles? Are we talking pets, here? Or, is it some kind of acronym? You know, like…quantum interference from bible belt yobbos? Not precisely quantum interference from bible belt yobbos, obviously, but something like it.

I'm saying: can you give me a clue, here? Something, anything to work with?

The Tech Answer Guy

Yo, Tech Answer Guy,

I think @baudrillardbitches is messing with you. I don't think that his messages mean anything – I think he's just typing in random letters and sending them to you.

Sincerely,
Helpful from Hamilton

Yo, Helpful,

Thanks for your input, but I don't think that's what's happening here. I think @baudrillardbitches' twits do have meaning, I just don't speak the lingo – dig? But, with a little help from @baudrillardbitches, I'm sure I'll be hip to the jive talk in no time.

The Tech Answer Guy remembers when he was a Little Tech Answer Guy, we used to make up our own language to be able to say things without the teachers knowing what we were talking about. Well, the other kids did. I was usually too busy building a piston engine or motherboard for a robot that shot lasers out of its elbows. But, now that The Tech Answer Guy is a little older and a little wiser, he knows the value of being able to communicate in one's own private language.

The Tech Answer Guy

Yo, Tech Answer Guy,

No, really, I think you're being played. I did a Googoo search for the term qibby, and it didn't come up with anything. Nothing. Not a single hit. You can type five random letters into Googoo, and it will usually come up with something! @baudrillardbitches is definitely making fun of you by making you look like you're – and I'm sorry to have to say this, Tech Answer Guy, because I'm a huge fan – old and out of touch.

Sincerely,
Helpful from Hamilton

Yo, Tech Answer Guy,

i don't say ur oaoot! no no no no no! ur fibulr! Abs strngix! dont listen 2 unHfH! he scotic!

Sincerely,
@baudrillardbitches from twatterville

Yo, Helpful,

You hear that? I'm abs strngix! Okay, so, maybe *you* don't understand the way new media is changing language, but I do.

A little. Well, okay, so maybe not that much, but at least I'm trying to understand what the kids these days are saying. Maybe some day you will join us.

The Tech Answer Guy

Yo, Tech Answer Guy,

I tried.

Sincerely,
Helpful from Hamilton

Yo, @baudrillardbitches,

Scotic? I think that's a bit harsh, don't you? HfH might be a little btt (behind the times - lol!), but that doesn't mean he deserves to be ridiculed like that. tomgw2tn (teh old must give way 2 teh new), but they should b gracious about it. After all, some day you will b the old person trying 2 understand what the younger generation is talking about. i have no doubt that you will want 2 be treeted with some modicum of respect then.

The Tech Answer Guy

Yo, Tech Answer Guy,

roflao!

Sincerely,
@baudrillardbitches from twatterville

Yo, @baudrillardbitches,

I know exactly what you mean.

The Tech Answer Guy

If you are a dude with a question about the latest technology, ask The Tech Answer Guy by sending it to questions@lespagesauxfolles.ca. Just remember: when The Tech Answer Guy says you can dis him, he doesn't mean that you can dis him. He means that you can dis him. Context is everything.

Ask Amritsar About the Proper Celebratory Emphasis

Dear Amritsar,

I know this guy. Tristan. I mean, I don't know him very well. And, I'm not sure if I did I would even like him. He's the kind of person who thinks Charlie Sheen is a good role model, you know?

Still, he asked me to be Farcebook friends with him, and I know Tristan well enough to know that he probably won't try to chop my head off with a soup spoon (what's going on in Brooklyn?) to have agreed. I just noticed that today is his birthday. I will probably wish him "happy birthday," but I don't want to give Tristan the wrong impression about how I feel for him. Should I use exclamation marks after that, and, if so, how many?

Isolde

Hey, Babe,

I was going to respond to your question, but the Language Corrector Dude raised his hand and said, "Ooh! Ooh! Ooh! I can answer this one! Let me! Let me answer this one!" He does that. Not having a column of his own, he wanders around the Alternate Reality News Service bullpen, looking over people's shoulders at what they are writing to see if he can "be of assistance." There's probably a column in that, but it wouldn't answer your question, so I will leave it for another time.

Since his expertise is actually appropriate in this instance, I figured I should give the Language Corrector Dude the opportunity to

Oh, thank you thank you thank you thank you thank

Ahem.

Right. Okay. Generally speaking, one exclamation mark is considered sufficiently restrained while 27 exclamation marks is seen as either an early sign of Tourette' Syndrome or an indication that the dosage of your medications is not high enough. If I were you, I would see my personal physician, or my personal OED editor.

This is simple enough; where it gets tricky is all of the potential combinations between one and 27. Each culture seems to have its own rules on the use of exclamation marks, as the partial list below indicates.

- In France, nobody believes you're being emotionally honest until you've used at least six exclamation marks!!!!!!!!
- In Afghanistan, if you use an exclamation mark, you will likely get shot by friends of your clan, but

if you don't use an exclamation mark, you will likely get shot by enemies of your clan!

- In Egypt, exclamation marks look like hieroglyphic birds.

- In Italy, three exclamation marks seems to be the norm, although this increases to 12 or more exclamation marks during the FIFA World Cup and, of course, exclamation marks have to be given up for Lent!!!

- In Estonia, two exclamation marks means: "I want to marry your yak!!"

- People in Ireland tend to avoid exclamation marks, because they start to spin in Irish eyes and eventually look like the doughnut of doom telling them to wait for their computer programme to finish whatever it is doing.

- Iraqis use four exclamation marks to celebrate the fact that it's one of the three hours a day in which they have electricity and can actually access their Farcebook pages!!!!

- In Mexico, the number of exclamation marks you use tells people which drug cartel you support! Unfortunately, because the situation is so fluid, this can change rapidly without notice!!

- In Fredonia, two exclamations marks means: "I want to offer you my yak's hand in marriage!!"

- In Eritrea, they use a single quote over a period because they cannot afford exclamation marks, so they tend to use them sparingly.

- Canadians who use exclamation marks are usually put under psychiatric observation for six to eight weeks (except for those who live in Alberta, who are rewarded for using exclamation marks with oil exploration grants)!!!!!

Quite the mish-mash – you could probably make a good side dish for baked koi with these rules! (NOTE: that exclamation mark was not intended to offend anybody in Denmark.) If you are uncertain about the appropriateness of exclamation marks in your email messages, consult you personal OED editor. Or, your personal physician. They're interchangeable, really.

Send your relationship problems to the Alternate Reality News Service's *sex, love and technology columnist at questions@lespagesauxfolles.ca. Amritsar Al-Falloudjianapour is not a trained therapist, but she does know a lot of stuff. AMRITSAR SAYS: expert guest columnists are a journalistic tradition; their presence should not be construed as an attempt by the author to get a column out with a minimal amount of work so she can devote more time to tearful conversations with her current partner about the division of their retro games collection while they are "taking time off from the relationship to reassess their priorities."*

Ask Amritsar About the Million Monkey March Madness

Dear Amritsar,

I am a three-time semi-finalist for the Pulitzer Prize for Best Moustache in a War Zone. My reporting on international affairs appears in the Alternate Reality News Service in 143 dimensions (and France). I was once hugged by Dame Priscilla Presley.

Despite my copious prestigiousness, my editrix recently asked me to write a story about a monkey with atomic powered prosthetic legs that, for some unknown reason, always seems to escape its owner en route to having amusing antics. Granted, when it puts on its elf ears and colourful waistcoat, it is adorable (in an aloof, we don't like the world any more so we are going to retreat from it kind of way); still, the Service has any number of less prestigiously advanced writers who would be happy to accept this assignment. Well, less unhappy, in any case. Why me?

I think I know what's going on, here. Management has subscribed to Zeitgeist Busters and Filigree, a service that synthesizes writing on more than half a million Web sites, social media apps and neighbourhood lampposts to find which of five million subjects are spiking in the public consciousness (like a bad fever, but without the owls running Parliament). ZBF told ARNS management that roaming monkeys would be popular in the next news cycle, so if we wanted to maximize eyeballs (not like Sauron, although that is always the first thing that I think of when somebody utters that phrase) we would have to get a story out on it right away.

News cycles (get into a frothy lather, rinse of nuance, repeat) are funny things. It seems to me that roaming monkeys have been the subject of four of the five last news cycles, knocked briefly off the front page by the invasion of the G'tar Shtryng of Anakronistes Four. (Which was unfortunate, because I really wanted to know if Earth managed to fight them off.) Because ZB&F's algorithm is proprietary (literally: in favour of the commander of an army or an elected magistrate), we don't know how they arrive at their suggestions; I suspect somebody in the company has an unusual fondness for upper primates.

Alas, alack and ala carte, adorable monkeys are to journalism what Tums are to Pink Floyd tribute bands: comfort food for intellectual anorexics. A journalist of my impeccable (I don't let birds anywhere near it) prestigiosity should not be asked to write articles on monkeys!

Is there any way I can get out of this assignment?

Name Withheld Owing to a Vindictive Editrix Who is Too Quick to Don the Slapping Gloves, If You Know What We Mean

Hey, Babe,

Are you sure you want me to answer this question? Don't you think it would be more advantageous for you to ask somebody with more business experience, like the Biz Whiz, or maybe your union rep?

Dear Amritsar,

You've been writing an advice column since 1947. This means that you are either: a) a bodiless head in a jar; b) a computer algorithm pretending to be a flesh and blood person, or; c) an ancient hag whose lifespan has been extended by unnatural means, scientific, necromantic or otherwise. Obviously, somebody who has been around that long must have accumulated wisdom on a wide variety of topics – I'm betting that this is one of them.

And, in any case, the Biz Whiz always reeks of cigarettes, even though he doesn't actually smoke. That just weirds me out.

Name Withheld so as Not To Get on the Biz Whiz' Bad Side Because Business Columnists are Notoriously Flaky and You Never Know When You'll Need Business Advice

Hey, Babe,

Okay, then.

Having been stung by the slapping gloves once or twice in the past myself, I can understand your dilemma. On the other hand, having been stung by the slapping gloves two or three (or more, let's be honest) times in the past, I'm not keen to repeat the experience. So, I would suggest that you swallow your pride and dance, monkey, dance.

And, thank you for the praise.

Send your relationship problems to the Alternate Reality News Service's *sex, love and technology columnist at questions@lespagesauxfolles.ca. Amritsar Al-Falloudjianapour is not a trained therapist, but she does know a lot of stuff. AMRITSAR SAYS: to be honest, the Biz Whiz probably would have given you the same advice. He knows which side his REIT is buttered on. If you really wanted an unexpected answer, you should have asked The Tech Answer Guy – he's an animal!*

Ask The Tech Answer Guy About the Profane
(He Doesn't Do Sacred.
It's a Thing With Him. Don't Ask.)

Yo, Tech Answer Guy,

I love hard liquor and easy women. I love that I don't even realize that that's a quote from a famous book because I've never read it. I love cars that go so fast they make the driver dizzy. I love movies that go "KA-BOOOOOOOOM!" I love language that could peel the paint off a rhinoceros' hide. I love meat wrapped in meat coated with meat with meat on the side (and, sometimes, a pickle – but, a big, meaty one!). I love summer, which allows me to enjoy two of my great passions: barbecuing the subject of the previous sentence and ogling the subject of the second clause of the first sentence in skimpy clothing. I love talking about the things I love, even when nobody wants to hear it. Especially when nobody wants to hear it.

Okay, now that I have proven my guy bona fides, you know what I really love? *Sailor Moon*. The magic. The schoolgirl uniform. Those big, round eyes. The schoolgirl uniform. The magic powers Serena gets when she puts on the broach and says the magic words. But, yeah, okay, mostly the schoolgirl uniform.

Anyhoo, I want to share my love of *Sailor Moon* on discussion boards dedicated to the kick ass anime character with the long blond hair. Unfortunately, this runs afoul (no pun intend – well, maybe a little pun somewhat intended) of my love expressed in sentence five from two paragraphs ago.

So. How can I indulge my love of *Sailor Moon* without compromising my masculinity?

Sincerely,
Tibor from Temiskaming

Yo, Tibor,

I know exactly what you mean. The Tech Answer Guy himself has fallen under the spell of *Mermaid Melody Pichi Pichi Pitch*. I, too, want to discuss it in appropriate places, and I, too, find myself expressing my admiration for it in inappropriate language.

One tactic that I have found efficacious is to substitute innocent, ordinary words for the naughtier ones I would ordinarily use. So, for instance, where I would use the word "ferk," I now use the word "flake." Snow comes in flakes. Cereal comes in flakes. Okay, flakes come in flakes, but, uhh, overall I think we can safely say that the word has more positive meanings than negative.

When somebody on the message board innocently asks why I responded to a post I disagreed with by writing, "Flake you!", I can say that I was merely suggesting that they eat some cereal. "Flake off?" It means remember to take some cereal with you when you leave the house. "Flakin' A!," I explain, means that I got a good mark in…breakfast studies.

Of course, not all scatological phrases translate equally well. I once had to explain that the phrase "I'll flake you legless," meant that I would force somebody to eat cereal until they were so fat that they could no longer walk. That was disturbing on a whole different level, one that was almost as inappropriate as the phrase I was trying to disguise.

That's not the only swear word you can use this way: I often substitute "shirt" for the word "shit." Many people respond to my use of the phrase "bull shirt" with LOLs and ROTFLs, conjuring up, as it does, images of cows in clothing. You and I may know that the phrase, "sad sack o' shirt" does **not** refer to a small bag of used clothes for the Salvation Army, but innocent readers don't have to know that.

Combining curses in this manner requires a certain amount of creative dexterity, but that's not to say that it can't be done. Consider a phrase like: "They were flaked up the apse." You and I know that that expresses a very naughty thought. However, for innocent readers of the discussion board, it can mean that some people had breakfast in the recessed area of the Church. Language doesn't get more appropriate than that.

Occasionally, this kind of word substitution will have the awkward effect of making an innocent phrase less so. "He'd give you the shirt off his back," when considered in this light, becomes rather disgusting. Overall, though, it is an excellent way to express your true feelings in venues where to do so would be highly inappropriate.

Or, you could find an adults only board to post to. Up to you.

The Tech Answer Guy

If you are a dude with a question about the latest technology, ask The Tech Answer Guy by sending it to questions@lespagesauxfolles.ca. Just remember: it's okay to snicker when somebody mentions caulking, but not so much that you actually allow leaks in your floors to undermine the foundation of your house.

Ask The Tech Answer Guy
About Putting That Disgusting Thing In Your Mouth

Yo, Tech Answer Guy,

Four years ago, I emigrated to Earth from Qwom (pronounced: Regigulous) as part of a corporate trade mission. As some of you may know, we Qwombats gave Earth plans for Shrievepark (pronounced: Drek) warp drives; in return, you gave us 20 DVD copies of the complete *Fawlty Towers*. (You originally wanted to give us 10 DVD copies of *The Best of Benny Hill*, but you clearly underestimated our mad haggling skillz (pronounced: skills).)

I will admit that adjusting to life on your planet was hard at first. It took me several months, for instance, to get over my revulsion at the fact that human beings wear their skeletons *inside* their bodies – I mean, how are you able to stand upright? And, how are you able to accomplish anything with only one thumb on each hand? (Qwombats may only have four digits per, but we're *all* thumbs!) Still, I was making great progress: I was able to interact with the humans in my office for several hours at a stretch without soiling my grefstrables. Much.

Then, I attended the company's ChristmaKwaanzUkah party.

I brought enough of my own liquid refreshment, distilled from the eggs of the Jubjub bird – they make a wicked Frumious Bandersnatch! – to share with several entities. Unfortunately, none of my human co-workers were tempted by the drink's deliciously sulfurous aroma, but, I wasn't offended. More for me, right?

Over the course of the evening, humans in black and white attire brought us trays of small edible things which they called "can of peas." At least, I think that's what they were called – my translator hiccoughed whenever the word was spoken, so I cannot be certain. Before I left Qwom, I had been warned to avoid human foodstuffs as our bodies are so dissimilar, which could make the ingestion of them quite unpleasant. However, my boss, Marisa Meckler, was scarfing down can of peas as fast as she could grab them off the trays, and insisted that they were so good that the rest of us had to try them – we just had to try them!

At first, I quoted famed physician Platz the Unforgiven on the genetic incompatibility between our species; unfortunately, the translation from the original Qwombish made it sound like I was complaining about your species' lack of body odour. When Marisa Meckler reminded me that my five and three sixteenths month assessment was coming up, I looked at the food on the tray and thought, *It's so small. What could eating one or two – or 16 – possibly hurt?*

Well! Eating a can of pea – or 16 – curled my carapace. That's not a euphemism for the effects of a strong alcoholic beverage, either: my back bent so badly that my head seemed to be permanently looking over my shoulder plate. As you can imagine, this gave me a new-found respect for peripheral vision! Of course, I couldn't explain what had happened without embarrassing my boss, so when co-workers asked if anything was wrong, you know, with my head, I explained that I was just going through puberty. A highly unexpected, somewhat delayed puberty for my species, but puberty nonetheless.

The effects of ingesting human food only lasted three Earth weeks, and I do not appear to have suffered any long-term damage. Unfortunately, next week there will be a retirement party for…somebody important in the office (I'm still a little hazy on the concept of corporate hierarchy), and I am afraid that my boss will pressure me into eating more can of peas. Or, worse, vanilla spongecake.

Can you recommend any way of avoiding this? Any way at all?

Sincerely,
Splorg the Unenviable from Calgary

Yo, Splorg,

You wouldn't believe how often I am asked this question. Not, this exact question, obviously; the Qwombatty Code of Frambleness (which, I gather, is similar to the human Macho Code of Manliness, except without the olive garnish) generally frowns upon asking alien species for advice. In fact, the only reason I'm not questioning your frambleness is that Qwombats have 13 genders, and trying to figure out which one you are and how badly you are violating Qwombatty social expectations of gender role performance is enough to give The Tech Answer Guy a very human migraine.

I just mean that most humans can understand having to choose between the desires of a superior in a social setting and avoiding the severe physical infirmity of giving in to the superior's desires in a social setting. Something about the combination of carefully non-denominational religious festivities and alcohol does strange things to the nervous systems of middle managers.

Unfortunately, there are no good solutions to this problem. You can't avoid going to the party, because your co-workers will think that you are sending information to the Qwom invasion force about the weaknesses in Earth's defenses. You can't piss off your boss because, frankly, most of Earth's galactic diplomatic corps grew up watching Three Stooges movies, so we really cannot afford an interplanetary incident. You can't even do the human solution of last resort: joining a monastery.

My advice: if you value your job, find a chiropractor who has experience with alien bodies!

The Tech Answer Guy

If you are a dude with a question about the latest technology, ask The Tech Answer Guy by sending it to questions@lespagesauxfolles.ca. Just remember: The Tech Answer Guy does not write the headlines for his articles. While he is sure that the poorly paid interns who do write the headlines won't be tempted to create anything rude just because they're bored and uncommitted to their jobs, he understands that there are no guarantees in life.

Ask Amritsar: Love, The Taxonomy
(Not The Tax Auditor)

Dear Amritsar,

What is love?

Mel N. Colea

PS: No, seriously.

Hey, Babe,

They say that Arctic peoples have 27 words for snow. This is, in fact, untrue: they only have three words for snow. As it happens, each word is 17 syllables long, and variable pronunciations and indifferent lexicographers have, over time, made it seem like there were many more.

Love is a four letter word, so you might reasonably expect that there aren't too many ways to pronounce it. You have clearly never attended a United Nations debate. Still, counter-intuitive though it may be, according to a study by researchers at the Poynter Sisters Institute, there are at least 7,327 distinct meanings for the word love in the English language.

According to the study, called *Fools for Love: The Original Title had 27 Colons and Was Three Pages Long, But the Publisher Deemed That Excessive, So We're Going to Leave it at That*, "a man might say that he loves his wife and he loves his car, but he wouldn't love them in the same way. At least, not without being begged to seek professional help." Authors Folger, Nescafe, et al suggested that new words be coined to deal with the different ways people use the word. These include:

- **loove**: love of traditional pets (ie: cats, dogs, rhesus monkeys);
- **luhve**: love of concrete;
- **looove**: love of edible objects smaller than a Volkswagen beetle's glove compartment;
- **lurve**: love of indie bands before they sell 100,000 albums or have a top ten hit (whichever comes first);
- **luurve**: love of non-traditional pets (dolphins, Komodo dragons, Reese's Pieces);
- **duhve**: love of soap;
- **(lo)^2(ve)^3**: love of alternate realities;
- **luuurve**: love of edible objects between the size of a Volkswagen beetle's glove compartment and a Volkswagen beetle;
- **lovie**: love of parts of the body you don't know the name of;
- **luves**: love of baby diapers;
- **loooove**: love of people who aspire to mediocrity;
- **lve**: love of special characters (except for ampersands and closed diagonal brackets);
- **luuurve**: the love of a woman for blowing raspberries into the toes of newborn babies.;
- **love** (pronounced l-ohve): love of the concept of technological determinism;
- **loive**: love of fairies, elves and pookahs;
- **lovoid**: love of curved surfaces;
- **lovey**: love of edible objects larger than a Volkswagen beetle;
- **lovana**: love of creepy pets (buzzards, black widow spiders, Anton Corbijn), and;
- **lovov**: love of bulleted lists.

Of course, everybody believes that their form of love is the purest, most profound expression of the emotion there is. But, really, who is to say that the love of slats (louver) is superior in any way to the love of fine art that you don't personally understand but feel deeply attached to because it seems like the thing to do (louvre)? Except, of course, for the love of aardvarks' eyebrows (lolove), which all reasonable people believe is icky.

Belief in the superiority of one's form of love leads to odd fracturing along geographic and temporal lines. For example, people who love American Supreme Court decisions before 1950 (lovve) cannot understand the passion of people who love Canadian Supreme Court decisions before 1950 (lovvve). Not only that, but neither of those groups has any respect for people who love American Supreme Court decisions since 1950 (vlove).

As if this wasn't confusing enough, the way Folger, Nescafe, et al conceive it, the same term can actually mean different things in different places. The word vloove, for instance, means the love of Spanish diacritical marks in the northern United States, the love of horseradish in the southern United States, the love of hourglasses with women's figures in northern England, the love of the worm at the bottom of the bottle in southern England and the love of personal mixed tapes in Poland. People who live in these areas are convinced that their use of the word is the only correct one. Families have split. Wars have been started. Academics have made tenure over the issue, and lesser people have been broken by it.

Given the huge number of ways in which the word is used, when you ask: "What is love?" I in turn have to ask: "Could you be more specific?"

Dear Amritsar,

I think it would be best if I joined a monastery.

Mel N. Colea

Hey, Babe,

Good move. You'll only be tempted by 57 different varieties of love there!

Send your relationship problems to the Alternate Reality News Service's *sex, love and technology columnist at questions@lespagesauxfolles.ca. Amritsar Al-Falloudjianapour is not a trained therapist, but she does know a lot of stuff. AMRITSAR SAYS: Howard Jones may have been no Wittgenstein, but, to be fair, old Wittie didn't perform at Live Aid, so, umm...there.*

Ask Amritsar: It Isn't Always About You

Dear Amritsar,

The other day, somebody posted a message on my blog that I wasn't fit to lick lonelygirl15's boots, and, even though I have no idea who that is, I got the distinct impression that I was being insulted. I wasn't sure what to do, so I consulted *Emily Post's Etiquette: Manners for a New World*. What she had to say was ve

Hey, Babe,

Let me stop you right there. You need to stop flossing with the laces of your boyfriend's tennis shoes, drop the dead donkey and programme your VCR to self-destruct if you ever watch Tom Cruise in any of his *Mission Impossible* reboots. Sometimes the right thing to do is the most obvious.

But, Emily Post? Seriously? You know, her first columns about interpersonal relationships were written on stone tablets, right? Seriously. The first question she answered was what to do when somebody sets your toga on fire in a vomitorium! (Her advice – do not get creative about putting out the fire, water works well – made sense, but still…) I know a lot of people adore her, but Emily Post was no lady! Did you know that she used to spit on the crowds that came to hear her play? That's right! Then, she stabbed her girlfriend Nancy to death, and died of a drug overdose before the trial started! And, she wore white before Easter! Not only that, but…umm…sorry, but I think I may have confused Emily Post with Sid Vicious. Yeah, yeah, that's what I did. Still, look at her record! This was the woman who told a distraught fremblotte from the planet Aristachus IV that if she wanted her griblings to stop making blastcytes at the dinner table, she/he/they/slothrop should serve garssloupes without first removing the crayatons! I know, right? You serve your griblings garssloupes without first removing the crayatons, and they'll just drop their moobleys right at the dinner fop. Then, then you have a real problem! (I would have advised her/him/them/slothrop to drop the griblings down a duragizer until they behaved, but nobody asked me…) Heavens to Mergatroid (Bert Lahr's second wife, not the villain from the ayeayePhone app *Star Blap: The Seriously Condensed Adventure*), how can you trust somebody who gives such unhelpful advice? Look, I'm not saying Emily Post killed my dog. Dale Carnegie's dirty paw prints were all over that one – he took influencing people way too seriously. I'm just saying that if you have a choice between somebody who died when computers took up a room and had bugs that were not metaphors for programming errors but were actual insects, or somebody whose entire career has been on the Internet, well, who do you think would be a better guide to life in the modern media-saturated world? You don't have to answer that – it would be me. Of course it would. Let me give you another example: according to Emily Post, you shouldn't talk on a cellphone while walking down the street because you might accidentally walk into a stranger. Ooh. Wouldn't that be awkward – walking into a stranger? Now, if you had asked me, I would say that you shouldn't talk on a cellphone while walking down the street because **the low level radiation will slowly turn your brain into cerebral stew**! Walking into somebody or feeding a family of four (non-zombies) on brain bouillabaisse – honestly, which do you think would be more awkward? Alright, I may have been a little melodramatic, there – the science doesn't really support the cortical dinner course conceit. Still, that just proves my point. Emily Post was writing in a simpler time, when you could pass off folk wisdom as something that had worked for millennia just because it had worked for millennia. Today, we back up our opinions with science. This gives modern advice columnists a solid grounding that previous generations of advice givers just didn't have. Even when we get the science wrong. Or, the science itself is proven wrong. Fortunately, in those cases, better science comes along to bail us out! It's time non-sciencey Emily Post passed the torch to a new generation of advice columnist. And, if she isn't willing to do that, I **will** wrestle the torch from her 50 year old corpse!

Send your relationship problems to the Alternate Reality News Service's *sex, love and technology columnist at questions@lespagesauxfolles.ca.* Amritsar Al-Falloudjianapour *is not a trained therapist, but she does know a lot of stuff. AMRITSAR SAYS: maybe I shouldn't write columns after drinking a dozen Fin Grizzlies, but advice columning is a vicious game. A vicious game. Mostly vicious. A game, maybe not so much.*

Ask The Tech Answer Guy Where the House Flies

Yo, Tech Answer Guy,

A few weeks back, I was selected to be a product tester for what I thought was a new brand of insect spray called Bug-B-Gone. It turns out the spray can actually produce a computer diagnostic display in midair. It's pretty cool, but I've run into some trouble with it. I tried to kill a fly with the spray before I knew what it was, and it seems to have created some sort of cyborg insect. The condition also appears to be contagious among the insect world. My question is this: how does one go about killing a horde of suddenly intelligent house flies?

Sincerely,
kaedance from teh Interwebz

Yo, kaedance,

Interesting name – is that Italian?

I'm afraid (which is, of course, merely a figure of speech – The Tech Answer Guy ain't afraid of nothing, believe it!) that, short of an EMP (not to be confused with an MP, an EMT or a PMS – especially a PMS), there isn't much you can do to get rid of your newly cybernetic flies (or cy-flies). They laugh at flyswatters. Really. Have you ever heard 100 sentient houseflies laughing? It's a sound that would make Jim Butcher become a vegetarian!

Bug sprays won't work; the cy-flies will just develop tiny gas masks (the speed with which they take ideas from R and D to production would make Silicon Valley jealous!). No Pest strips are worse: when there are enough cy-flies, they'll put your cat up there in their place. Not only will this not rid you of the sentient houseflies, but it will make the cat even more of your mortal enemy than it already is.

Talk about a lose-lose situation! (Lose-lose-lose if the tension of the situation causes you to drop some weight. Do be aware, however, that the American Medical Association – Long Beach Branch does not recommend the Mordor Cy-fly Tension Diet.)

Having cy-flies in your home isn't all bad, though. For one thing, they are attracted to piezoelectric materials (so-called because the atoms are arranged in the shapes of pies and made up of sub-atomic particles with the flavours apple, strawberry-rhubarb and Spring Day in Ireland). Simply commission a sculpture in the shape of a bowl of fruit, a bust of Beethoven or a bottle of bikini wax, plug it in and voila! Kinetic art!

Or, if you prefer, you could coat some of the surfaces in your home with chocolate. When cy-flies land on the chocolate, they get stuck. When enough of them are caught in this way (*The Cybernetic Apocalypse Cook Book* recommends at least six cy-flies per square inch), use a spatula to take them to a baking tray and put them in an oven at 350 degrees for 45 minutes. The results are a delicious dessert that is high in protein. (Or so I'm told. On the advice of my gastroenterologist, The Tech Answer Guy only eats stone-washed Belgian truffles.)

If your family does not enjoy cy-fly brownies, you can always bring them out late at night when you want party guests to get the hint that it's time to go home.

Over time, of course, the cy-flies will multiply. When there are enough of them, you might consider turning your house into a tourist attraction, like a butterfly sanctuary, only with houseflies. (Of course, if the Smith-Yamashitas next door also have a cy-fly problem, you could end up in competition for tourist dollars. You might want to consider commissioning a sculpture made out of piezoelectric materials in the shape of the main street of your city; the flies moving around inside it would be an attraction the Smith-Yamashitas couldn't compete with! And, if you sold cy-fly brownies in the gift shop, you could make even more money out of the...problem may be too strong a word. Let's call it a plague.)

No? You don't like the tourist attraction option? What ever happened to this country's entrepreneurial spirit? This is why China is eating our strawberry-rhubarb piezoelectric materials for lunch!

Eventually, the air in your house will be so thick with cybernetic houseflies that you will no longer be able to live in it. This terminal phase is actually a good thing. Pushing against the ceiling, they will eventually dislodge your house from its foundation and fly into the air with it; at that point, it will become the Air Force's problem!

Then, you can rebuild. And, as you're laying the foundation for your new home, you will always read the instructions on bug sprays before you use them. Right? RIGHT?

The Tech Answer Guy

If you are a dude with a question about the latest technology, ask The Tech Answer Guy by sending it to questions@lespagesauxfolles.ca. Just remember: girls are also welcome to submit questions to The Tech Answer Guy. They, uhh, they are just considered honourary dudes for the duration of the column.

Ask The Tech Answer Guy About the Meet of the Matter

Yo, Tech Answer Guy,

Our neighbours are good people. Kind people. They have never sold bootleg *Little Big Man's Planet* DVDs to minors. They don't bulldoze slum properties sending hundreds of people to live on the streets in *Get a Life*...not with their official avatars, in any case. They still feed their Tamagotchis long after the rest of the world has moved on to another generation of fad technologies. Or, five.

However, in the dozens of times Krffplitz and Mbellonium have entertained us over the last 15 years, all they've ever served for dinner is orange glop with lumpy bits. My wife, Edwina, assured me that this was different from the green glop with lumpy bits that she used to serve when we were first married, and I must admit that it has an aftertaste of plutonium that never graced my wife's cooking. We strongly suspect our neighbours are serving us a vegetarian dish, although we have both wondered, without telling the other, if it may, in fact, be alien food.

Regardless of what the FBI lab ultimately says it is, my wife and I are agreed that we do not want to eat our neighbours' meals any more. We have tried to deal with this matter without actually, you know, being honest about how we feel. In case they're sensitive about it, you understand. I'll never forget that aftertaste of plutonium, though. Never.

Once, we brought t-bones to their house as a treat; not only did our neighbours look at the steaks like they had never seen such a thing before, but, a couple of days later, we found Krffplitz using them to wash his car.

Another time, we offered to take our neighbours out for dinner. Despite the fact that they seemed enthusiastic about a night out, no matter what we suggested – Chinese, Thai, Stockholm archipelagoan – they refused. In the end, we went to a place that they raved about and, wouldn't you know it, it was probably the only place in town – if not this side of the galaxy – that specialized in orange glurp.

We don't want to hurt our neighbours feelings. They're kind people. Decent people. People who may have ray guns. But, if we have to eat any more orange goop, my wife and I may just have to burn their house down. What should we do?

Sincerely,
Eldon from Edmonton

Yo, Eldon,

Ordinarily, The Tech Answer Guy refers all questions not relating to technology to the Department of Circular Filing, if you catch his (meaning: my) drift. However, today is your lucky day, because it just so happens that one of the exceptions to this rule that he (meaning: I) makes is for questions involving meat or meat products; and, in any case, this question has special relevance for him (meaning: me) because he (meaning: what, do I have to repeat myself?) has some personal experience that might be relevant here.

I'm not allowed to divulge any details until all of the lawsuits have made their way through the tailors, but, I can say that in a situation similar to yours, The Tech Answer Guy faked food poisoning.

It was actually pretty easy once I got the idea. I just stayed home for a couple of days and, the next time my friends asked me and Mrs. The Tech Answer Guy to dinner, I pointed out that they had given me food poisoning the last time I ate there. After that, they felt so guilty that they were putty in my hands (an unfortunate choice of metaphor considering that that's what the food they served us tasted like).

Mrs. The Tech Answer Guy thought the whole thing was suspicious: "I don't remember you throwing up or anything," she pointed out. I told her I wretched quietly because I didn't want to interrupt her watching *Coronation Street*. She had always said that she had wanted The Tech Answer Guy to be more considerate of her feelings, so what could she do? She melted.

Some people may find my methods a little…extreme. However, extremism in the pursuit of meat is no vice, if you know what The Tech Answer Guy (meaning: The Tech Answer Guy) means!

The Tech Answer Guy

If you are a dude with a question about the latest technology, ask The Tech Answer Guy by sending it to questions@lespagesauxfolles.ca. Just remember: burning down a neighbour's house is not an action that should be taken lightly. Be sure to use safety matches.

Ask Amritsar: The Ideal You (Give Or Take)

Dear Amritsar,

You know how, when people are nervous about meeting others for the first time, they are told: "Just be yourself?" This is good advice **if you're Mother Teresa**. Unfortunately, since most of us aren't Mother Teresa (probably including Mother Teresa), this advice is about as helpful as "Look both ways before you cross a loan shark" or "When in doubt, throw the clown a porcupine!"

Let's be honest: people aren't always the best judges of how to promote themselves to others, especially potential mates. Why would a man put at the top of his match.com profile that he has the biggest collection of tarantula corpses in the province? I mean – just, why?

That's where I enter the picture (one of those moving ones that you see in Harry Potter). For over a decade, I have worked as a match site "adjuster." People pay me to edit their online profiles on sites like eHarmony and Zoosk to make them appear more appealing to people they hope to meet. This is how it works:

ORIGINAL POST: If I like your photo, I will stalk you.

ADJUSTED VERSION: Enjoys getting to know new people.

To be able to get through my day without having to drink a fifth of Scotch, I convinced myself that this wasn't helping people be dishonest. Oh, no. I was helping people express the Platonic Ideal of who they were.

Over the years, these are some of the Platonic Ideals I have helped people discover about themselves:

- laughs like a disturbed pack mule = heartily enjoys a good joke
- high school dropout = self-educated
- spends all of her free time playing computer games = is easily amused

- has a large porn collection = has a fine appreciation for the human form
- drives a used car = collects vintage automobiles
- prone to manic depression = sees life from both sides
- spends all of his free time reading bodice rippers = has a romantic spirit
- writes poetry = ? (I haven't quite been able to crack this one. "Is artistic" is generic and comes with its own baggage. "Good with words" could come across as glib. "Is quick with a rhyming dictionary" is, at best, a gamble. I try to discourage clients from using this on their profiles.)
- is a right wing Internet troll = has good communications skills
- picks nose = has a keen interest in nasal hygiene

I have never had to use the last one, but in this business it pays to be prepared.

Somewhere between prone to manic depression and spends all of his free time reading bodice rippers, my Platonic Ideal of what **I** was doing began to fray around the edges. I wondered what it would be like if I went on a date with somebody whose profile said he "plays well with others" only to have him ask to borrow money because the profile actually meant that he had a gambling problem. I suspected I would not be happy. I started to think that Plato drank a fifth of Scotch to get through **his** days.

I tried telling myself that my job was no different from the seller describing his home as unstressful, with lots of room for pets and a great basis to build upon when he really means that it's dreary and has bats in the attic and a crumbling foundation. Except for the exterminator bills, I suppose.

Still, you can't kid Margot Kidder. Lately, I've begun to worry that there is no difference between freshening up people's profiles and not being forthcoming...shading the truth...lying. Other than the big commissions, I suppose. Am I responsible for the disappointment of the person who thought they were getting a partner with a keen interest in nasal hygiene feels when they find the person not living up to his Platonic Ideal?

Can you help put my mind at ease on this subject?

Daria Verpeake

Hey, Babe,

People who are lonely brood. And, people who brood do one of two things: go on a rampage and shoot others from a bell tower or make maudlin movies about the impossibility of emotionally connecting to another human being. The way I see it, if you can keep even one lonely person from making a maudlin movie about the impossibility of emotionally connecting to another human being, your entire life will have been worthwhile.

Send your relationship problems to the Alternate Reality News Service's *sex, love and technology columnist at questions@lespagesauxfolles.ca.* Amritsar Al-Falloudjianapour *is not a trained therapist, but she does know a lot of stuff. AMRITSAR SAYS: when you believe in things you don't understand...and you stutter? Stevie, what are you trying to say?!*

Ask the Tech Answer Guy About The High Cs

Yo, Tech Answer Guy,

Can you please explain the difference between causation and correlation?

Sincerely,
Aristotle from Ajax

Yo, Ari,

Umm…pfffffft – you got me. How many beers you've had that evening?

The Tech Answer Guy

Yo, Tech Answer Guy,

I can't believe you blew off Aristotle's question like that. Do you have any idea who he is? Naah – me neither. Still, he's a mortal…probably…he certainly seems Greek, and that gets him halfway there, and, well, anyway, he asked a straight question so he deserves a straight answer.

Causation and correlation – what's the diff?

Sincerely,
Plato from Pickering

Yo, Plats,

Yeah, well, you know, The Tech Answer Guy *could* respond to the question – it's not like you've stumped him or nothing.

But, it just so happens that The Tech Answer Guy had taken his chopper – the Harley Roller – in to Phil, the mechanic from the shop down the street and idly brought up the question while he was filling a tire with completely coincidentally low air pressure. And, as it happened, Phil, the mechanic from the shop down the street – who is really smart for his pay grade – put it better than The Tech Answer Guy ever could.

According to Phil, the mechanic from the shop down the street, correlation is what happens when you notice that the onboard navigation system of your Specific Motors Rabid Lemur starts spitting out routes for traveling through the Andromeda star system at the same time as the ratchet housing of the ball bearing crankcase springs a leak. Causation, on the other hand, is what happens when you believe that the onboard navigation system of your Specific Motors Rabid Lemur spitting out routes for traveling through the Andromeda star system **has caused** the ratchet housing of the ball bearing crankcase to spring a leak.

There. I couldn't have put it better myself. Trust me on that one.

The Tech Answer Guy

Yo, Tech Answer Guy,

Umm, yeah. I'm sure that that answer is profound to people who eat motor oil for breakfast and know who won the 1900 Gordon Bennett Cup (formally titled the I Coupe Internationale). But, for those of us who maybe don't love our cars too much, can you please translate that answer into English?

Sincerely,
Socrates from Sudbury

Yo, Socks,

Yeah. Yeah. Okay. I can, umm, do that. Sure.

Correlation is when you...uhh...notice that your cat is coughing up furballs at the same time that...that...and, this is the really clever bit – at the same time as your neighbour threatens to call the fire department because the smoke from your summer barbecue is setting off alarms in his house...half a block away. Causation, on the other hand, is what happens when you – what did I say? – when you believe that your cat coughing up furballs is the cause of – sorry, **is the cause of** your neighbour threatening to call the fire department because the smoke from your summer barbecue is setting off alarms in his house...half a block away.

Easy peasy queasy sneezy.

Oh, and, I happened to run into Phil, the mechanic from the shop down the street, being questioned by police in regards to certain unauthorized middle-of-the-night auto body customizations, and he told me that Fernand Charron won the 1900 Gordon Bennett Cup (formally titled the I Coupe Internationale). Smart guy, that Phil, the mechanic from the shop down the street.

The Tech Answer Guy

Yo, Tech Answer Guy,

You don't really understand the difference between correlation and causation, do you? It looks like you just mimicked the form of what Phil, the mechanic from the shop down the street said. Anybody can do that.

Correlation is what happens when you notice that you sneezed at the same time as the heat death of the universe. Causation is what happens when you believe that your sneeze **caused** the heat death of the universe.

That doesn't really prove anything, does it?

Sincerely,
Aristotle from Ajax

Yo, Ari,

Seems to me that you busting my balls over this question is caused by the fact that you've been dead for over 25 hundred years. How's that for causation, pal?

The Tech Answer Guy

If you are a dude with a question about the latest technology, ask The Tech Answer Guy by sending it to questions@lespagesauxfolles.ca. Just remember: being necrotic does not mean that you get a thrill from staring at other people's necks. Please stop trying to use the language to justify your creepiness. Oh, and, you might want to cut back on watching True Blood.

Ask Amritsar To Share Her Jocular Attitude

Dear Amritsar,

Can you please use your cutting wit on me?

Anna-Julianna Ananda

Hey, Babe,

No.

advertisement Glomper's Chompers: the nuclear
powered dentures that give you a 50
gigawatt smile! advertisement

Dear Amritsar,

Oh! I'm sorry! I didn't mean to imply that you were in any
way insensitive to your readers! You only use cutting wit on
people who are deluded, people who really know what their
problem is, but do not seem capable of admitting it to
themselves. In short, people who deserve – oh!

Anna-Julianna Ananda

Hey, Babe,

Was that a...an advertisement? Seriously? Brenda, Tell me
that I'm wrong, that that wasn't an advertisement!

[BRENDA   BRUNDTLAND-GOVANNI: Umm...you're
wrong. That wasn't a, umm, you know, advertisement.]

advertisement NEW at Tim Horton Hears a Who:
break pad crullers. Tastes great, and,
when installed in your hovercraft, gets 35
millimetres to the calorie! advertisement

Dear Amritsar,

I...I've done kind of a...bad thing. My robopet Phyllis (he's a cross between a cocker spaniel and a giraffe) was almost seven, which is 1,784 in human years, and he was going a little...senile. Instead of scanning the morning papers for articles I would be interested in, Phyllis piddled in my cornflakes. Instead of scanning the TV for shows I would want to watch, he piddled on the converter. Instead of chasing his ball in the park when I threw it, Phyllis piddled on a Rottweiler.

Granted, Phyllis' piddle smelled like strawberries and forgotten dreams of youth; still, when it's all over the house (and parts of the neighbourhood, and neighbours' pets – especially neighbour's big, angry pets), the scent tends to lose its emotional resonance. And, I'm allergic to strawberries.

I wasn't ready to let Phyllis go, though, so I...I took him to a Pet Semenary.

Anna-Julianna Ananda

Hey, Babe,

Advertisements in the middle of an advice column? Really, Brenda, this is outrageous! In fact, this is far outside the boundaries of rageous!

[BRENDA BRUNDTLAND-GOVANNI: I'm sorry, Am, really, I am, but the marketing department has found that people pay no attention to ads around articles. In fact, readers pay negative attention to those ads: they imagine that space is taken up by images of gigantic alien space squids fighting battle cruisers in the Oort cloud. Seriously. The marketing department's research is **very** detailed. The only way marketing could see to make our online offerings pay was to insert the ads directly into the copy. And, I shouldn't have to remind you – despite the pleasure that doing so gives me – this income is part of what pays your salary.]

Dear Amritsar,

People warned me against leaving Phyllis at the Pet Semenary, but I was desperate not to lose him, and I thought if anybody could help him with his decaying logic routines and faulty memory circuits, it would be somebody who hadn't lived outside a place of quiet, meditative contemplation for several decades.

After an absence of a week, there was a scratching on the window of my bedroom on the third floor. (Cockeraffes have really long necks.) It was Phyllis! He had returned to the family! I was overjoyed. Until I noticed that his eyes were a strange shade of vermillion, but I shrugged that off as a sign that he was happy to be home.

It didn't take long for strange things to start happening in the neighbourhood. People found their morning newspapers were delivered with letters cut out of the headlines, while my family received notes about our computer caches being kidnapped if we didn't leave batteries in a brown paper bag in a garbage can in a nearby park. Wifi towers were sprayed with graffiti that featured eyes on a really long neck looking over a wall and read "Killjoy was here." One morning, everybody for three blocks found their car radios had been turned to a local techno station.

Clearly, the Phyllis who returned from the Pet Semenary was not the one I had left there the week before.

How long should I continue living in denial before, in a frantic middle of the night melee, I have to decapitate Phyllis with a vinyl LP my ex-boyfriend – who, I am now strong enough to admit, is a music snob – just happened to leave around the house?

Anna-Julianna Ananda

Hey, Babe,

Need I remind you that my contract has a no interruptions of my writing for fire, flood, political assassination, act of god **or advertisements** clause?

[BRENDA BRUNDTLAND-GOVANNI: You want to do that? Really? Lawyers is the direction you want to take this in? Because, frankly

advertisement TWEETEDIT: Because life's too short to waste reading bad Tweets. Really short. Over before you even know it. So, say "Pah!" to bad Tweets. advertisement

Oh, wow. That really was annoying, wasn't it? Ferking advertisements think they can interrupt **me** do they? Well, we'll just have to put a stop to **that!**]

Dear Amritsar,

So, umm, about my problem?

Anna-Julianna Ananda

Hey, Babe,

First, I don't wit on demand.

Second, you expect me to respond to an advice column letter writing wannabe whose fabrications don't rise to the level of a warmed over Stephen King plot? You've shown about as much creativity as a three legged bolintar running the Falouppian Marathon in a space suit and high heels! Get back to me when you have a real problem!

Dear Amritsar,

Thanks! You're the greatest!

Anna-Julianna Ananda

Hey, Babe,

Don't mention it. Please.

Send your relationship problems to the Alternate Reality News Service's *sex, love and technology columnist at questions@lespagesauxfolles.ca. Amritsar Al-Falloudjianapour is not a trained therapist, but she does know a lot of stuff. AMRITSAR SAYS: confession is good for the soul, not the sole. Theologians are divided on the question of whether or not fish have eternal essences, except, for some reason, for groupers, because, as the title of the film truly tells us,* All Groupers Go to Heaven. ˎ

Ask the Tech Answer Guy to Explain Himself

Yo, Tech Answer Guy,

I know that you profess to follow the Macho Code of Manliness, but I sometimes get the sense that you are trying to reach beyond it to a deeper understanding of life, the universe and every Ting Tings. Is that true, and, if so, what is your deeper understanding?

Sincerely,
Lydia from East Phlamydia

Yo, Lydia,

You got me.

I don't talk about it much, but I developed some theories of human behaviour when I was doing my Masters in Psychology. (Relax, guys: in accordance with the Macho Code of Manliness, I flunked out...after I received my degree. My relationship with the bursar was complicated.) The one that has stuck with me all this time is that all of the problems that men have can be traced back to our relationships with our fathers.

You think the artificial intelligence that controls all aspects of the spaceship that is taking you to Saturn has started to kill your fellow crewmembers? Not at all. Your problem is that your father was too strict when you were growing up. Having doubts about your own humanity as you do your job tracking down and terminating astonishingly lifelike androids in artfully decaying Los Angeles, doubts that could get you killed? Nyuh unh. Your problem is that your father wasn't strict enough with you when you were growing up. Swept up from the desert planet where you grew up to fight in a galactic war, but uncertain that you can get beyond your rational training and embrace the quasi-mystical philosophy that will allow you to complete your mission? This one should be obvious! Your father was a traveling rodeo clown who scared his own children, traumas they're still working through as adults.

Get the idea?

The problem with totalizing theories is that they can become boring very quickly. Having trouble figuring out how to weaponize an alien organism that just wants to kill your entire species? It's not because what you're trying to do is insane. It's because your father was never around when you were growing up. You're trying to implement a genius' blueprint for ultimately peaceful galactic psycho-historical development, but unaccounted for anomalies threaten to upset the plan? It's not because life is full of unexpected developments that are beyond our control. It's because your father doted on you too much when you were young, smothering your creativity. You have to deliver information that has been uploaded into your brain and have it removed before it kills you? Isn't it obvious? Your father read a book on "good parenting" and did all of your disciplining while standing on his head, and you're still trying to come to terms with your confusion.

Now, heaven and Brenda Brundtland-Govanni forbid that I bore my readers, so, when somebody asks me a difficult question, I answer by making shit up. It's really clever shit, very authoritative sounding. Some of it is based on the Macho Code of Manliness, of course; the rest blends Freud with *Popular Mannix*. And, who knows? If my theory about fathers is wrong, the shit I make up is as likely to be true as anything else.

The Tech Answer Guy

Yo, Tech Answer Guy,

Is that true?

Sincerely,
Sam from Nam

Yo, Sam,

Not a word of it. Weren't you paying attention to the part about making shit up?

The Tech Answer Guy

Yo, Tech Answer Guy,

According to rule 27 of the Macho Code of Manliness, and I quote: Everything in the world is black and white. Real men don't eat ambiguity.

Unfortunately, I find "a lot of ambig"uity in today's column. (Sorry about the quotes – they drifted.) So, what's it gonna be – you make up shit or you don't?

Sincerely,
Alphonse from Beyonce

Yo, Alphonse,

Yes.

The Tech Answer Guy

If you are a dude with a question about the latest technology, ask The Tech Answer Guy by sending it to questions@lespagesauxfolles.ca. Just remember: The Tech Answer Guy recently...put out his...back. Yeah, that's it. His back. Was put out. He was...rescuing...a...a kitten that had gotten stuck up a – in a – at the bottom of a gravity well. A kitten stuck in a well. That's how he put out his back. And, long story short – not, we would like to make clear, that the Alternate Reality News Service has anything against tall people, we're just sayin' – The Tech Answer Guy's doctor has been experimenting with the dosages of his meds. So, if he seems a little...different, cut the guy some slack. Did we, uhh, did we mention he was saving a kitten?

Ask Amritsar: That Was the Whole Point, Wasn't It?

Dear Amritsar,

As I approach my ninetieth birthday, I find more and more that I ask myself the same simple question: was I ever loved, truly loved?

Babette

Hey, Babe,

Yes.

Send your relationship problems to the Alternate Reality News Service's sex, love and technology columnist at questions@lespagesauxfolles.ca. Amritsar Al-Falloudjianapour is not a trained therapist, but she does know a lot of stuff. AMRITSAR SAYS: I reserve the right periodically to be sincere.

ALTERNATE INDEX

Ask Amritsar...

ABOUT THE AUTHOR

Ira Nayman once shot a man in 3-D just to watch him dye.

Okay, okay, Ira Nayman is the author of one novel; he has also self-published five collections of Alternate Reality News Service (ARNS) articles in print. "The Weight of Information," the pilot for a radio series based on ARNS articles, can be found on YouTube. He updates his Web site of social and political satire, *Les Pages aux Folles* (www.lespagesauxfolles.ca), with new writing and cartoons on a weekly basis. Ira won the 2010 Swift Satire Writing Competition.

Oh, and, as you may have noticed, he is not above puns.

ALSO BY THE AUTHOR

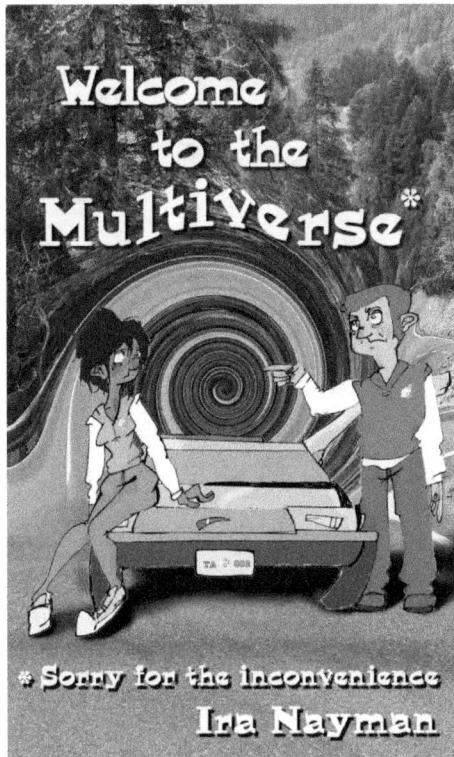

*Welcome to the Multiverse** is the first novel by the creator of the Alternate Reality News Service! Noomi Rapier, fresh out of the Alternaut Academy, joins with veteran Transdimensional Authority investigator "Crash" Chumley for her first case. But is she ready to confront…herself?

"[O]ne of the funniest sci-fi books I've ever read." (Seregil of Rhiminee, *Rising Shadow*)

"Welcome to the Multiverse is a cracking read that almost had me in stitches, fresh and original humour from a comedy genius." (Antony Jones, *SF Book Reviews*)

* *Sorry for the Inconvenience*

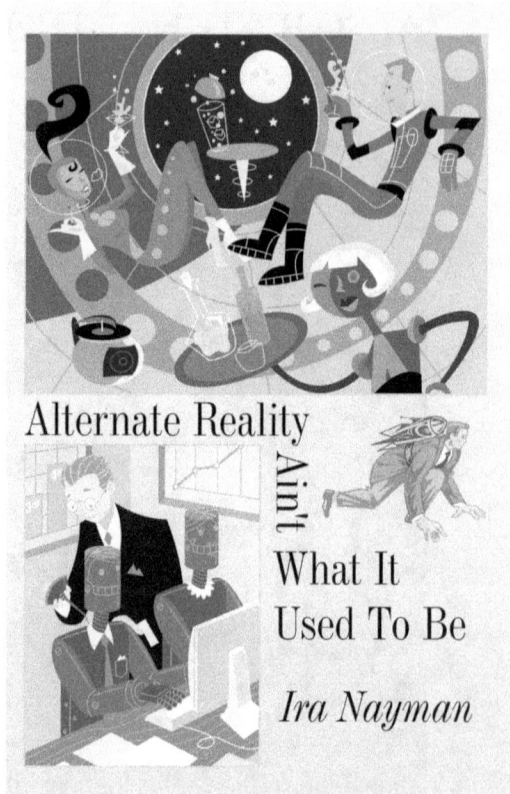

A woman is sued for alimony…by her AI enhanced service android! High school history class is proven conclusively to be boring…by science! The United States government thinks it can end the war in Iraq by allying itself with…the Democratic Union of Great Old Ones (a rebranding of demons from another dimension)! All this and so much more can be found in *Alternate Reality Ain't What It Used To Be*, the first Alternate Reality News Service book!

"[O]ne of my favorite books of 2008…" (Charles de Lint, *Fantasy and Science Fiction Magazine*)

"Ira Nayman has a genius for pulling zany ideas out of the ether and populating his books with them." (Geoff Nelder, *The Compulsive Reader*)

THE ALTERNATE REALITY NEWS SERVICE
Ira Nayman, Proprietor
If you don't like this reality, try another!

What Were Once Miracles
Are Now Children's Toys

Giant heads appear over monuments throughout the world…and France! War between the United States and China is averted…because the Asian country repossesses America's military to pay off its debts! Attempts to recreate wooly mammoths from fossilized DNA are successful…except they're the size of a small housecat! The multiverse gets stranger in *What Were Once Miracles Are Now Children's Toys*, the second collection of Alternate Reality News Service articles.

"Nothing is without the potential for humor in Nayman's mindset, and he twists, puns, and snarks his way through the morass of human life, helping us laugh at the sometimes utterly ridiculous world around us. Be prepared to laugh when reading *What Were Once Miracles Are Now Children's Toys*." (John Ottinger III, *Grasping for the Wind*)

Luna for the Lunies!, the third collection of Alternate Reality News Service articles, features: a poem about a violent coffeemaker; an app that sends teens a fake phone call when it appears that they are about to get lectured by their parents, and; a report on the expedition to find the Chinese butterfly that is causing hurricanes in the United States. If you don't like this reality, try another one…or another 80!

"Ira takes a wickedly dry sense of humor and rips apart the popular culture, politics, and technology of our modern world through a series of satirical articles that range in size from a handful of sentences to pages in length, and believe me when I say that no one and nothing is spared. It is a laughter inducing indictment of our society and I loved it." (Eric Swett, *My Writer's Cramp* Web site)

www.ingramcontent.com/pod-product-compliance
Lightning Source LLC
LaVergne TN
LVHW051456080426
835509LV00017B/1774